DATE DUE

4-28-17 IL: 174087015			

Managing Marginal School Employees

Applying Standards-Based Performance Measures

Lynette Fields
Brianne Reck
Robert Egley

Rowman & Littlefield Education
Lanham, Maryland • Toronto • Oxford
2006

Published in the United States of America
by Rowman & Littlefield Education
A Division of Rowman & Littlefield Publishers, Inc.
A wholly owned subsidiary of
The Rowman & Littlefield Publishing Group, Inc.
4501 Forbes Boulevard, Suite 200, Lanham, Maryland 20706
www.rowmaneducation.com

PO Box 317
Oxford
OX2 9RU, UK

British Library Cataloguing in Publication Information Available

Library of Congress Cataloging-in-Publication Data

Managing marginal school employees : applying standards-based
  performance measures / by Lynette Fields, Brianne Reck, and Robert Egley.
     p. cm.
  Includes bibliographical references and index.
  ISBN-13: 978-1-57886-407-2 (hardcover : alk. paper)
  ISBN-13: 978-1-57886-408-9 (pbk. : alk. paper)
  ISBN-10: 1-57886-407-0 (hardcover : alk. paper)
  ISBN-10: 1-57886-408-9 (pbk. : alk. paper)
  1. School employees—Rating of—United States. 2. School personnel
management—United States. I. Fields, Lynette, 1964– . II. Egley, Robert,
1956– . III. Reck, Brianne, 1959– .
LB2831.58.M36 2006
371.2'02—dc22   2005033016

♾™ The paper used in this publication meets the minimum requirements of
American National Standard for Information Sciences—Permanence of
Paper for Printed Library Materials, ANSI/NISO Z39.48-1992.
Manufactured in the United States of America.

Contents

Preface

The demand for highly qualified, well-trained educational leaders has never been higher than it is today. In an era of high-stakes accountability, teacher shortages, enormous external pressures, and increasingly complex role expectations, educational leaders must possess a variety of knowledge and skills to successfully support student learning. Among the chief and most difficult challenges facing today's school administrators is supervising instructional and noninstructional employees who, for any number of reasons, fail to carry out their responsibilities efficiently and effectively. By some estimates, between 5 percent and 15 percent of teachers in 2.7 million public education classrooms are marginal or incompetent (Tucker, 2001). And while no statistics reflect the full impact that marginal teachers, administrators, and noninstructional staff have on student achievement, the importance of instructing educational leaders to deal effectively with these individuals is evident.

This collection of case studies is designed to give readers an opportunity to grapple with real-world scenarios that call for problem solving, ethical action, and a demonstration of the knowledge and communication skills used by successful administrators on a daily basis. This work acknowledges the paradigm shifts and redefinition of the knowledge and skills needed by today's educational leaders. In its introduction to instructions for implementing standards for advanced programs in educational leadership, the National Policy Board for Educational Administration (2002) identifies five broad areas in which current thinking diverges from the traditional knowledge base in educational leadership and previously held expectations regarding the role of building-level administrators. Those shifts are from technical skills to interpersonal skills, from director to consensus builder and motivator, from resource allocation to accountability for learning processes and results, from campus administrator to integrator of school and community services, and from policy recipient to policy participant. Since personnel issues are often the most emotionally charged and time-intensive problems confronting administrators each day, our intent is to prepare prospective or in-service administrators to face the challenges they will encounter in their leadership positions. We do this by providing opportunities to have the virtual experience of sitting in the decision-maker's chair and supervising marginal faculty, staff, and administrative personnel.

This book provides situations drawn from today's schools. It is organized to encourage readers to assess and develop their knowledge and skills in the areas identified by the national standards for educational leadership developed by the Educational Leadership Constituent Council and recognized by the National Council for Accreditation of Teacher Education. *Please note, however, that while the scenarios contained in this book were inspired by both our and our colleagues' supervisory experiences, the cases have been fictionalized, so any resemblance of the characters to any persons, living or dead, is purely coincidental.*

Each chapter focuses on a critical area identified by the standards and has an introduction to situate the scenarios presented in context. The cases selected for each chapter are designed to guide the readers through the process of making theory to practice connections as they analyze the situation presented, identify possible strategies, and weigh the potential intended and unintended consequences of various courses of action. Each case is accompanied by a set of questions to guide reflection and discussion and suggested activities to extend learning.

As a teaching tool, *Managing Marginal School Employees* provides professors of educational leadership and professional development providers with a primary or companion text to engage administrative candidates or practicing administrators in problem-based learning that addresses the challenges of human resources management. The cases have been field-tested in graduate-level courses at a research university, are aligned to national standards, and are intentionally concise yet open-ended to support flexible group discussion or individual reflection. The realistic scenarios cross grade levels and settings and present complex challenges that call upon the readers to analyze situations and to synthesize and apply their knowledge of theory, policy, and ethical considerations to make judgments and choose appropriate strategies to resolve real-world conflicts. As we prepare a new generation of educational leaders to face diverse sets of challenges, it is our hope that this book will provide a tool for developing the decision-making skills of the individuals whom we will count on to make schools safe and effective places for teaching and learning.

This book is most suitable for graduate courses in the field of educational leadership, including:

- Principles of administration
- Supervision
- Human resources
- School law
- Problems in curriculum
- Principalship
- Conflict resolution
- Administrative analysis and change

REFERENCES

National Policy Board for Educational Administration (2002). Standards for advanced programs in educational leadership for principals, superintendents, curriculum directors, and supervisors: http://www.npbea.org/ELCC/ELCCStandards%20_5-02.pdf.

Tucker, P. J. (2001). Helping struggling teachers. *Educational Leadership* 58(5) 52–55.

CHAPTER 1

Professional and Ethical Leadership

Educational Leadership Constituent Council Standard 1—Professional and Ethical Leadership specifies that candidates who complete the program are educational leaders who have the knowledge and ability to promote the success of all students by acting with integrity, with fairness, and in an ethical manner.

The typical ethical heuristic and imperative for educational leaders is "to do the right thing because it is the right thing to do." For the inexperienced school administrator, discerning the right thing in the face of competing interests and expectations in an unfamiliar context can be more difficult than one might expect. While professional standards, personal belief systems, and school district policies frame choices and offer theoretical guidance, there is no substitute for reflective practice and the development of an ethical code that an effective leader demonstrates every day. This ethic is not reserved for significant decisions in time of crisis but becomes evident over time in routine decision making, such as that regarding the use of resources, time, and curriculum development (Lashway, 1997). The current context of public education creates a unique set of challenges that make it both critical and difficult for leaders to develop a strong and consistent personal code of ethics that inspires trust and enables them to provide leadership.

Given the exacerbated pressures created by high-stakes accountability and the increasingly complex nature of their roles, school leaders must exhibit character and integrity to build trust and implement change

(Sergiovanni, 1996). Such times and circumstances call for transformational leadership to create conditions for change. Burns (1978) states,

> Transforming leadership is elevating. It is moral but not moralistic. Leaders engage with followers, but from higher levels of morality; in the enmeshing of goals and values, both leaders and followers are raised to more principled levels of judgment. . . . Much of this kind of elevating leadership asks sacrifices from followers rather than merely promising them goods. (p. 455)

A leader must develop a personal and professional moral compass and seek to influence the culture of a school or organization. This critical sense of direction must be evident to others, and it will be tested as the leader works with marginal employees to improve the learning opportunities and outcomes for students. The educational leader must assume the role of the "first citizen" of the school community. She or he sets the tone for the way in which employees interact with one another and with members of the school, the district, and the greater community. An effective leader must develop an ability to examine his or her own personal and professional values that reflect a code of ethics. As role models, school leaders must accept responsibility for using their position and its attendant power and authority ethically and constructively to ensure that all students are served.

In this chapter you will be asked to consider several scenarios that call for you to exercise critical thinking and ethical decision-making skills. As you wrestle with the dilemmas presented, consider the personal and professional values and ethical standards that inform your efforts to act fairly, ethically, and with integrity to resolve conflicts and provide leadership in the school setting. After responding to each case study and engaging in the suggested activities, develop a statement that reflects your personal platform and the code of ethics that will guide you in your leadership decision making and actions.

CULTIVATING GROUP NORMS

Problem 1: Stealing Is Stealing—
A Custodian Who "Borrows" School Supplies

You are the principal of a school. One of the secretaries comes to see you. She says that she used the copy machine after Mr. Abbott, a night-time custodian. He left some of his originals in the machine. She hands the originals to you, and you notice that the documents are children's Sunday school lessons and activities. Later that same day, you receive a telephone call from a parent. The parent says that her child is in Mr. Abbott's Sunday school class. When she went to pick up her child from Sunday school yesterday, she noticed several school items in the church classroom such as a stapler, paper cutter, and scissors with your school's name on them. When the parent questioned her child about the school supplies, the child said, "Mr. Abbott told us not to worry about it—he said that the principal gave him permission to use any necessary school supplies for our Sunday school classroom." Mr. Abbott has been at your school for eight years. Up to this point in time, Mr. Abbott's evaluations have been "satisfactory."

Case Questions

1. What do you say to the secretary?
2. How do you respond to the parent?
3. How are you going to investigate this matter?
4. If Mr. Abbott has used school supplies for his Sunday school class, how will you deal with this?
5. If Mr. Abbott deceived others about your approval of his use of school supplies for his Sunday school class, how will you respond?

Suggested Activity

Interview three school administrators. Ask them what disciplinary action they believe is appropriate for Mr. Abbott if he used school supplies for his Sunday school class and lied to others, saying that he had the principal's permission to do so. Write a short paper (three to four pages, double-spaced) that summarizes your interview findings. Furthermore, describe why as an ethical principal, you must address the situation.

Problem 2: The David Forman Story—
An Assistant Principal Who Lets the Cat out of the Bag

In June, you and your administrative staff—David Forman, assistant principal, and Carry Brown, guidance counselor—are working on the next year's class assignments. All of you are randomly assigning the students to classrooms, as the school board policy for your district clearly states that you should do. After several days on this task, a group of concerned parents, a few influential teachers that are well respected in the community, and a new school board member come to see you. Unknown to you when they arrived, Mr. Forman had disclosed to one of the persons in the group that you were randomly assigning students to classrooms. At first the group of parents, teachers, and the board member are exchanging pleasantries. They tell you how proud they are to have you as their new principal. As the meeting progresses, the group of parents, teachers, and the board member begin to share with you "how things were done" under the former principal's twenty-year tenure and how much he was loved and adored as the principal. Then the questions start pouring in about why you have decided to change the former principal's long-standing tradition of allowing parents to select their child's teacher.

Case Questions

1. As principal, you chose to follow school board policy. Was doing so a good idea? Why or why not? Defend your answer.
2. If you had discovered that Mr. Forman had told the group about the random assignment without regard to parental choice, how would you have handled it?
3. What are the major historical, philosophical, ethical, social, and economic influences that may have affected the reaction of those who came to see you?
4. Identify and critique several theories of leadership and their application to this situation.
5. How should you respond?

Suggested Activities

1. Develop a short list of questions and comments that you think this group might throw at you.
2. Write a short paper (three to four pages, double-spaced) explaining how you would facilitate the development and implementation of a shared vision and strategic plan that you can use with

your administrative team to reduce the likelihood that the work you are doing will be communicated to others in the community.

MAINTAINING A PROFESSIONAL CODE OF ETHICS

Problem 3: An Assistant Principal Caught with His Pants Down

You are the superintendent of a school district. On Sunday afternoon, you receive a phone call from one of your principals, who is very upset. She tells you that she saw one of her assistant principals, Michael Ranzinni, on the Channel 9 news. Michael is an outstanding assistant principal who is well liked and respected. On Saturday evening, he was at the local mall and was arrested in the men's public restroom for indecent exposure. The local police department set up a sting operation where a male police officer posed as a person soliciting sex in the public restroom. You check the local newspaper and find the same story on the second page.

Case Questions

1. What are the legal implications of this situation?
2. What are the ethical issues of this situation?
3. What actions should you handle personally to de-escalate any potential concerns of parents, students, coworkers, and community members?
4. What actions will you delegate to the principal to de-escalate any potential concerns of parents, students, coworkers, and community members?
5. If Mr. Ranzinni is guilty of a crime, what are the disciplinary options?
6. If Mr. Ranzinni is innocent, how could you assist him in protecting and restoring his reputation?

Suggested Activity

Consult the school statutes in your state. If Mr. Ranzinni is guilty of indecent exposure, a misdemeanor, how could this affect his teaching and administrator certification in your state?

Problem 4: Lying, Cheating, and Taking Credit for Others' Work— An Untrustworthy Assistant Principal

You are the principal of a school. One of your assistant principals has retired, and you receive a phone call from the superintendent asking you to accept Ms. Washington as a transfer from the district office. You accept the transfer and, within a month, three faculty members whom you have known for several years each make an appointment to see you. The first faculty member, a guidance counselor, tells you that she does not want to work with Ms. Washington in organizing and administering the schoolwide standardized test next year. You ask why. She says that when she worked with her this year, Ms. Washington did not attend any of the meetings and did none of the work. You are surprised because Ms. Washington gave you the impression that she handled testing personally. The second faculty member, who is one of your best math teachers, tells you that Ms. Washington does not support him when he writes discipline referrals. He states that he wrote a discipline referral for David Smalley. David had been disruptive in class and, when called to task, became belligerent, disrespectful, and used profanity. Ms. Washington did not take any action on the referral and, according to David and David's mother, said that the teacher tends to exaggerate. When the teacher confronted Ms. Washington, she told him that she gave the student in-school suspension, of which, according to the teacher, the student never served one day. The third faculty member is one of your science teachers who is chairing the committee for the school science fair. She comes to you because Ms. Washington asked to be a judge for the fair. When Ms. Washington evaluated the science projects, she gave first-place awards only to girls. According to some students, she winked at a couple of the girls and said, "You don't have a thing to worry about."

Case Questions

1. What relationship should principals and assistant principals have?
2. Do you accept what the faculty members have said at face value, or do you investigate further? If so, how?

3. What will you say to the faculty members who brought their concerns to you?
4. If Ms. Washington has lost the trust of some faculty members, how serious of a problem is this? Why?
5. What do you say to Ms. Washington?
6. Do you involve the superintendent? If so, how?

Suggested Activity

Write a short paper (three to four pages, double-spaced) that describes how the situation could affect the school culture. Furthermore, describe what you believe to be the best solution to improving school culture in this particular situation.

Problem 5: Is the Principal Sleeping with His Secretary? Dealing with Rumors

You are an assistant principal. Your principal, Mr. Robinson, has shared with you that he has been closely supervising and working with two marginal teachers. These teachers are vocal about what they perceive to be unfair treatment by the principal and have solicited the support of others. One day after school, Ms. Wang, one of the marginal teachers, drops by your office. She chitchats for a while but then confides in you that she knows that the principal, who is married, is having an affair with his secretary. Ms. Wang believes that Mr. Robinson wants to get rid of her because she knows that he is having an affair. You have observed that Mr. Robinson seems close to his secretary, but you have never seen any inappropriate behavior.

Case Questions

1. How do you respond to Ms. Wang?
2. If you choose to investigate this matter, how will you do it?
3. Why would you choose not to investigate this?
4. What, if anything, do you say to your principal?
5. Should you contact anyone at the district office? If so, who?

Suggested Activities

1. Find out what action (legally or within the district) could be taken against someone who spreads a false rumor.
2. In your district, find out what type of protection there is for an employee who thinks that they are being disciplined out of revenge.
3. Write a short paper (three to four pages, double-spaced) that summarizes what you found and how you as an assistant principal would handle the situation.

Problem 6: The Emperor's New Clothes—A Principal Who Can't Handle the Truth about His Performance

You are an assistant principal of a new middle school, and you are responsible for the direct supervision of instructional staff on one grade level. A first-year language arts teacher comes to you with several concerns about his perceptions that teachers at the various grade levels appear to be treated differently by the principal. He reports that many of his colleagues have privately voiced similar opinions but are reluctant to approach the administration. You share the teacher's concerns with the principal in a private conversation. He angrily dismisses the teacher's concern as being groundless. The next day, the principal distributes a survey instrument seeking teacher feedback on their perceptions of the opening two months of school and their feelings about the culture, the climate, and the level of administrator support they have received. The first-year teacher responds to the anonymous survey frankly, raising questions and pointing out inconsistencies between the principal's espoused and enacted values and behaviors. The angered principal goes on a rampage, attending team and department meetings, stridently demanding that teachers either confirm or refute the opinions expressed by the anonymous survey response, challenging the faculty as a whole to provide evidence to support the concerns raised, and asking for the name of the disgruntled teacher. Faculty member response is consistent. Teachers in these meetings either remain silent or disavow any knowledge of any differential treatment. The first-year teacher, in an effort to clarify his responses and correct the principal's misperceptions, schedules a meeting with the principal and yourself, identifies himself as the respondent, and tries to offer an explanation for his observations and survey response. The principal listens stonily and, when the teacher leaves, comments that he will not have disloyal troublemakers in his school. One week after the incident, the principal calls the teacher into the office and documents the conference with a letter to the teacher's file, citing alleged instructional deficiencies and outlining an improvement plan. Despite consistent positive feedback from students, parents, and colleagues and outstanding evaluations and observations from his immediate supervisor (you), the curriculum specialist, and the director of middle schools, the teacher is notified in December, three weeks after the incident and two weeks after the development of the assistance plan, that his contract will not be renewed. For the rest of the year the teacher is hounded by the principal, who refuses to review the improvement portfolio submitted by the teacher or reconsider his decision to nonrenew.

Case Questions

1. What effect might the principal's conduct have on the teacher (e.g., what are the emotional and physical consequences for the teacher?), and how might such conduct affect the teacher's classroom instruction and student learning?
2. What are the foreseeable consequences of this situation and the principal's conduct on school climate and culture?
3. Under your district's policies and state and federal laws, what actions can the teacher take?
4. What actions can you as an administrator take, and what professional standards and ethical considerations might guide your actions in response to this situation?

Suggested Activity

After considering professional standards of conduct and your personal philosophy of education, create a supervisory philosophy outlining the parameters that will shape your actions in a supervisory role.

REFLECTIVE QUESTIONS

1. What are your core leadership values that drive how you make decisions?
2. What are the organizational norms, values, and beliefs of your school?
3. What are the organizational norms, values, and beliefs of your school district?
4. How prepared are you as a professional and ethical leader?
5. What do you need to do to improve your abilities as a professional and ethical leader?

REFERENCES

Burns, J. M. (1978). Leadership. New York: Harper & Row.
Lashway, L. (1997). Ethical leadership. ERIC Digest, Number 107. Eugene, OR: ERIC Clearinghouse on Educational Management.
Sergiovanni, T. J. (1996). Leadership for the schoolhouse: How is it different? Why is it important? San Francisco: Jossey-Bass.

CHAPTER 2

Information Management and Evaluation

Educational Leadership Constituent Council Standard 2—Information Management and Evaluation specifies that the institution's program prepares school leaders who demonstrate an understanding and capability of:

- Conducting needs assessment by collecting information on the students; on staff and the school environment; on family and community values, expectations, and priorities; and on national and global conditions affecting schools
- Using qualitative and quantitative data to inform decisions, plan and assess school programs, design accountability systems, plan for school improvement, and develop and conduct research
- Engaging staff in an ongoing study of current best practices, relevant research, and demographic data and analyzing their implications for school improvement
- Interpreting educational data, issues, and trends for boards, committees, and other groups, outlining possible actions and their implications

Data-driven decision making is the currency of the realm in the high-stakes accountability atmosphere in which we currently find ourselves in public education. Administrators often complain that they spend more time creating graphs, charts, and reports representing student achievement than they do in working with teachers to facilitate and support student learning. Similarly, every new silver bullet program is touted as "research based" and framed as "best practice." For the novice administrator, making sense of the barrage of information, selecting and utilizing accurate and appropriate data to make instructional decisions, and knowing what data to gather and analyze can be daunting.

A school leader who seeks to implement change must not only gather student achievement data but weigh the potential benefits and liabilities associated with any course of action selected to address the realities described by the data. Understanding the limitations of the picture painted by test data alone, knowing the capacities of the faculty and staff to implement change, and communicating effectively with stakeholders affected by any planned course of action is critical. As with any efforts to make informed improvement in schools, there are intended and unintended consequences associated with each choice. The marginal employee adds an additional dimension to the decision-making process and often presents challenges that call for a highly integrated capacity to gather and analyze data and to make appropriate decisions to ensure that students are well served and that a school continues to function efficiently.

In this chapter you will consider scenarios that ask you to examine the implications of decisions involving both instructional and noninstructional matters and to think about ways in which you might gather, utilize, and communicate information to your internal and external publics about good instructional practice, facilities management, and the nature and implications of change. As you consider each challenge and determine the ways in which you might address the issues raised by the examples, you will want to take note of the potential intended and unintended consequences that might follow from various actions or strategies. Keeping the goal of ensuring student success should help to guide your decision making.

ANALYZING AND USING DATA

Problem 7: The Nonexample—A Principal Who Pushes Change Too Quickly

You have taken an attractive early retirement package from New York's public school system as the superintendent of a large district and have moved to Florida. You apply for the vacant principal's position in the area in which you have decided to make your retirement home. Much to your surprise, you are selected as the school board's unanimous choice.

You are eager to get started and have contacted several colleagues that you believe would be strong candidates for the vacant administrative positions that are currently open at your school. Several colleagues indicated that they would like to apply and that they would welcome the opportunity to work with you again.

You recommend two of your former colleagues who have proven track records for improving tests scores in their former schools in New York. The board approves them as new hires for the district with the understanding that test scores will continue to improve.

Upon the arrival of the new administrators, you give them the power and authority to do whatever it takes to improve student achievement as evidenced by improved tests scores on the state assessment test. Before the teachers return for the new school year, you and your administrative staff institute new reading and math programs, order new textbooks, purchase scripted lesson plans for each subject area, and arrange for a four-day-long in-service for all teachers on how to use the new curriculum and resources.

When the teachers arrive, they are furious about the changes that have been made without consulting them. The teachers feel disrespected and marginalized as professionals and request a meeting with the principal and administrative staff. During the meeting the teachers provide evidence that the tests scores have been improving over the last several years and that all the schools in the district have made adequate yearly progress, according to the state's. The spokesperson for the teachers asks the administrators what information they used to make such radical changes. The spokesperson for the teachers asks the administrators to justify the large expenditures for the new reading and math instructional programs, the new textbooks, the scripted lesson plans, and the in-service provided by the creators of these programs.

Case Questions

1. How will you justify or defend you decision to make radical changes without consulting the teachers?

2. What should you and your administrative staff have done before making changes to the instructional programs?

3. How will you and your administrative staff deal with the faculty, knowing that they feel disrespected and marginalized by the decisions that were made without their input?

4. How might the superintendent and school board be adversely affected by the decisions made by you and your administrative staff?

5. What are some pros and cons of making curriculum and instruction decisions without seeking input and buy-in from the faculty responsible for implementing these programs of study for the students?

6. How might this politically charged curriculum and instruction decision affect the supervision and performance appraisal of the faculty?

Suggested Activities

1. Select a curriculum issue at your school that you believe needs to be changed or improved. Gather, analyze, and interpret educational data and trends for this issue at your school. Develop an action plan for possible events to address this issue. Describe the implications of the action plan on current practices and the possible effects on school culture.

2. Identify the types of qualitative and quantitative data that you would use to make informed decisions, plan and assess current school programs, and plan for improvement in the area of student achievement.

Problem 8: I Taught It Once; They Did Not Get It. I Must Move On!

You are the new principal of a school that has many excellent teachers. Improving student achievement has always been a concern, but the last three administrators were either unwilling or unable to deal with marginal teaching performances. You were hired because of your reputation for having high expectations for students and teachers and for having the courage to deal with ineffective teachers.

Students, parents, teachers, and even former administrators have identified Mr. Rogers, an experienced teacher, as displaying common behaviors of ineffective instruction that have negative implications on student learning. To list a few, Mr. Rogers is known for failure to create an appropriate classroom atmosphere, lack of personal insight and motivation, failure to monitor student comprehension and understanding of concepts being taught, and an arrogant unwillingness to accept responsibility for problems. Unfortunately, Mr. Rogers has become used to receiving satisfactory evaluations in the past.

During the first six weeks of the school year, the complaints about Mr. Rogers begin to mount. You and your administrative staff meet with Mr. Rogers. You inform him that you and your staff will closely monitor his teaching practices. You schedule formal and informal observations of his teaching during various times of the week and day, which yield evidence that the complaints you have been receiving are accurate.

Throughout one observation you hear Mr. Rogers tell his students that twenty out of thirty-two students failed the last test and that they had better buckle down for the next test or they are in jeopardy of failing his class. You leave a note on Mr. Rogers's desk as you leave the room. The note asks him to see you during his planning period and that he should bring his grade book to the meeting.

During the meeting with Mr. Rogers, you question him about the statements he made about the number of failures on the last test and ask him how many students are currently on track to pass his course. Mr. Rogers proudly displays his grade book and shows you that over 75 percent of his students are doing poorly and will likely fail his course. You ask Mr. Rogers if he ever considered reteaching subject matter when many of the students did not master it. He informs you that he doesn't have time for remediation. He states that he taught the subject matter once. According to Mr. Rogers, if the students don't get it, he must move on because he has so much more knowledge to impart. Mr. Rogers brags that he has a high failure rate because the students are just lazy and do not care.

You ask more questions of Mr. Rogers and discover that his instruction has many problems that must be addressed immediately. You and your administrative team inform him that he will be placed on a plan of improvement. His resistance is quite obvious, but he agrees to do the best that he can.

Case Questions

1. What type of information or data will you and your administrative staff collect about Mr. Rogers?
2. From whom will the information be collected?
3. How will you use the information to guide your actions to help Mr. Rogers improve his instruction?
4. Justify your decision to place Mr. Rogers on a plan of improvement.
5. What are the next steps that you and your administrative staff will implement to monitor Mr. Rogers's instructional practices?
6. If Mr. Rogers chooses to tell other faculty about his plan of improvement, how could this affect school culture?
7. What strategies will you and your administrative staff implement to maintain positive school culture when working with someone like Mr. Rogers?
8. How could Mr. Rogers's past satisfactory teacher evaluations affect your current plan of improvement for him?

Suggested Activities

1. Develop and explain the needs assessment that you and your administrative staff might conduct to get a handle on the ineffective instructional practices that Mr. Rogers must correct.
2. Describe the types of data, issues, and trends that you might uncover during the intensive plan for improvement for Mr. Rogers that can be used to help other teachers within your school.

Problem 9: Just Not Management Material—
The Inept Head Plant Operator

You are a new principal at a middle school. There are approximately fourteen hundred students and eighty-five faculty and staff at your school. You have an undersized lunchroom and must run five lunchtimes a day.

The current head plant operator has been at your school in his current position for one year. Prior to being a head plant operator, he was an evening custodian, and his evaluations were good.

Within the first two weeks on the job, you notice that your school facility is not well kept. The floors are dirty and lack shine. The classrooms are dusty, and the windows look like they have never been cleaned. The cafeteria has exceptionally dirty walls, with pieces of food permanently stuck to the ceiling. Some of the tables and benches are falling apart.

The grounds are in worse shape than that of the facility. Pieces of paper are everywhere. The weeds are overtaking the flowerbeds, and the sidewalks have debris on them.

Many of the teachers have complained to you about how dirty their classrooms are. Your superintendent drops by for a visit and makes a comment that she knows you are going to quickly address your "custodial issues."

Case Questions

1. How would you respond to your teachers?
2. What would you say to your superintendent?
3. Where will you begin in addressing your custodial issues?
4. What, if anything, do you say to the head plant operator at this time?
5. What, if anything, do you say to your custodial staff at this time?

Suggested Activities

1. Develop a needs assessment to determine the current status of your custodial issues. Describe how you will collect information from students, faculty and staff, parents, and, in particular, the custodial staff. Explain how you will mentor the head plant operator in establishing expectations and priorities for his staff.
2. Develop a checklist for the disposition of the campus so that you or your head plant operator can easily document the appearance and functioning levels of different areas of your school facility.

BEST PRACTICE AND RELEVANT RESEARCH

Problem 10: Longer School Days—Say What?

Betty Hayseed, curriculum coordinator of the New Horizon School District, presented a proposal to the superintendent that suggested that the district lengthen the school day by sixty minutes beginning next school year. Betty had prepared an elaborate research and literature review supporting her claim for such a decision. Her research included powerful statements about time on task, academic learning time, engaged time, various learning styles, brain-based learning strategies, and theory related to multiple intelligences.

The superintendent listened and read the volumes of research-related materials that Betty put together. He asked many questions of her to determine the level of her commitment to such a change in the daily schedule. She withstood the endless challenges that the superintendent posed to her. The superintendent told Betty that he felt confident that overall the district would demonstrate significant gains on the Iowa Tests of Basic Skills if the district implemented longer school days. He also expressed his hope that this change might appease the Board of Education and the public that were pushing for academic excellence.

The superintendent had some concerns but thought that Betty had sufficient research to support her recommendation. Noting that some considerations may need to be addressed, the superintendent gave Betty permission to proceed. He suggested that she meet with the principals and school improvement committees to get their input.

Case Questions

1. Assume that you proposed what Betty proposed. Describe other stakeholders that you would want to talk with before going any further. Why would this be important?
2. Do you think student achievement is directly related to lengthening the school day? Why? Why not?
3. What type of action research project could you pilot to determine the effect of lengthened school day on student achievement?

4. Based on your experiences, what factors other than the ones high-lighted by Betty might influence student achievement?
5. What are some alternatives that might be considered to promoting improved student achievement?
6. What issues will the teachers have with this proposal?
7. What type of union concerns could arise?
8. What concerns might the parents have related to the proposed changes in the length of the school day?

Suggested Activities

1. Develop and explain the needs assessment that Betty would be wise to consider before making such a recommendation. Be sure to include information collected from students, staff, family, and community, and address the impact of such a decision on all the stakeholders.
2. Analyze and interpret current research findings on the lengthening of school days. Use your findings to support or refute Betty's recommendation.

Problem 11: The Unhappy Parent Volunteer

You are a new principal. Two of your teachers come to see you during their break. Ann is a first-grade teacher, and Ray is a second-grade teacher. Ray complains that a parent volunteer, Ms. Glum, comes to his room three times per week and challenges his teaching methods. The parent has also been critical of his fairness when dealing with some of his students. Ann provides some background information for you as she supports the complaints made by Ray. Ann explains that she had Ms. Glum's son last year and that the parent demonstrated some of the same behaviors when she volunteered in her room.

You ask Ray for specific details. Ray explains that he often provides assistance to students who are unable to complete tasks independently and that he leaves the other students to work on independent practice. Ms. Glum's son, Brian, is one of the students that comprehends the lesson presented and gets right to work on the assignment or project. Ray explains that Ms. Glum has strongly protested his method and claimed that he is ignoring her son's educational needs. Ray tells you that he attempted to explain his method of instruction to Ms. Glum but that she was not satisfied. Ann states that she experienced the same type of complaints and pressure from Ms. Glum last year.

You ask Ray if there is any other issue that you need to know about. Ray indicates that he has one other teaching method to help the lower-performing students that drives Ms. Glum up the wall. You ask Ray to proceed. Ray explains that he often provides the poor readers with a list of questions to guide them to important information or to remind them of important steps to follow when reading. Ray explains that when he uses this strategy, Ms. Glum protests that he is being unfair to her child and all the others who did not receive the same treatment. Ray assures you that he tried to explain his methodology to her concerning this complaint, too. Ray adds that he has asked her to set up a meeting with the second-grade lead teacher to discuss her concerns. Ms. Glum told Ray that she was going to see the superintendent and that he can forget the lead teacher and the principal because she knows they will cover for his inadequate teaching abilities. Ann concurs with Ray: She tells you that Ms. Glum did the same thing to her last year.

Case Questions

1. Is Ray on solid ground with his teaching methods? Why or why not?
2. What type of data or research would be helpful in determining the effectiveness of Ray's teaching methods?
3. What would you say to Ray?
4. Assume that the parent went to the superintendent. Predict what he will do. Then explain how you will respond.
5. What would you say to Ann?
6. Would your comments to Ann be of significance to other teachers on your staff? Why or why not?
7. What action plan would you put into place to address this problem?
8. How would you find out if there have been similar problems with parent volunteers at your school?

Suggested Activities

1. Research the literature on parental involvement and volunteers in schools. Develop a parent volunteer handbook or guide that is based on current best practices and relevant research.
2. Identify available data from your district related to parent involvement and school volunteerism. Describe what type of qualitative and quantitative data you would use to make changes in the present policy or process based on the potential problems identified in the case study.

Problem 12: Homework for Elementary Students— Too Much or Not Enough?

You are the principal of an elementary school that has high test scores and a history of producing high-performing students as measured by the high-stakes testing program mandated by the state. You have above-average teachers and have given them great academic freedom to do "whatever it takes" to keep the students performing at the highest levels.

Ms. Scoffield, a third-grade teacher, has a policy of giving homework every night. It takes the students approximately one hour to complete, and it is collected every day. Ms. Scoffield grades the homework with letter or percentage grades, and all homework counts for 30 percent of the student's overall grade.

Another third-grade teacher, Ms. Dixon, has a homework policy that students are to spend no more than thirty minutes per night on homework. She grades homework as either *satisfactory* or *unsatisfactory*, and students can redo and correct their homework. In her class, homework counts for 10 percent of the overall grade.

A parent, Mr. Vest, has twin daughters. One of his daughters is in Ms. Scoffield's class, while his other daughter is in Ms. Dixon's class. Mr. Vest comes to you and expresses a concern about the major inconsistencies between the two teacher's homework policies. He explains that this situation is causing him major grief at home because his daughter in Ms. Scoffield's class cries about her homework almost every night. Mr. Vest tells you that he has a hard time explaining the fairness of this issue to his child.

Case Questions

1. As principal, can you support both of these teachers' homework policies? Please explain why or why not.
2. Is there one teacher's homework policy that you prefer over the other? If so, why?
3. What are some suggestions that you can make to teachers about their homework policies for their grade levels or departments?
4. Do you recommend or support districtwide policies that govern homework? Explain your reasoning.
5. How would you respond to Mr. Vest?

Suggested Activities

1. Review the research literature related to homework for elementary students. Analyze and interpret the research, and outline a schoolwide policy of homework for grades K–3 and 4–5.
2. Conduct a literature review on student motivation related to teaching and learning. Analyze and interpret the research. What does the research indicate on the variables such as intensity, direction, and duration? What research on student motivation might help support one of the homework policies over the others?

REFLECTIVE QUESTIONS

1. What needs assessment instruments are readily available for your use in assessing
   a. Student needs and progress
   b. Faculty/staff needs and progress
   c. Your school's environment
   d. Level of parental involvement
   e. Level of community support
   f. Impact of your leadership abilities on others
2. Of the instruments available to you, to what extent are you familiar with or comfortable using them and analyzing the results?
3. What professional development can you take advantage of to improve your skill set in the area of needs assessment?

4. Are you more comfortable using qualitative data or quantitative data? Please explain.
5. How up-to-date are you regarding national and global conditions affecting schools?
6. How would you engage your faculty and staff in an ongoing study of current best practice and relevant research?
7. What do you need to do to improve your abilities as a manager and evaluator of information?

CHAPTER 3

Curriculum, Instruction, Supervision, and the Learning Environment

Educational Leadership Constituent Council Standard 3—Curriculum, Instruction, Supervision, and the Learning Environment specifies that the institution's program prepares school leaders who demonstrate the knowledge, skills, and attributes to design with others appropriate curricula and instructional programs, develop learner-centered school cultures, assess outcomes, provide student personnel services, and plan with faculty professional development activities aimed at improving instruction.

It is fashionable to speak of building-level administrators as *instructional leaders*, but that term is being redefined in the age of accountability and high-stakes testing. The demands of the twenty-first-century school are different from those faced by administrators just a few short years ago. The sophisticated knowledge and skills needed by an administrator dedicated to ensuring high achievement for each child and for every child go beyond reviewing lesson plans and completing classroom observation checklists. Knowledge of effective teaching practice must be coupled with the ability to create a productive, inclusive, supportive learning environment that provides quality educational experiences for every student.

Communicating high expectations and providing the support, resources, and supervision are necessary but are not sufficient to ensure student success. Visions of academic excellence must be the motivating forces that drive our work. An effective leader recognizes that the classroom teacher is at the heart of all efforts to improve instruction. Supporting the individual and collective growth of teachers as self-motivated, self-regulated professionals is one of the most critical tasks of the administrator as a supervisor. Despite current trends toward standards-driven curricula and assessments, teachers are engaged in making curriculum and assessment decisions on a daily basis. They need guidance, support, and appropriate resources to do their jobs well. True instructional leadership provides useful constructive feedback about teaching performance, support for active involvement in the development of a quality curriculum, and opportunities to develop professional skills.

Compared to what we had in the past, we now have a more profound understanding of the importance of school culture and learning environments. Issues of diversity, achievement gaps, special learning needs, and high-stakes accountability have redefined the landscape. Effective educational leaders must be able to create a school culture that supports the work of teachers in their efforts to improve student achievement. This task is not something that they can do alone. Bringing teachers, families, and community members and resources together is critical. All partners in the process must learn to respect hard work and value student success. Accordingly, leaders must ensure that the learning environment in every classroom throughout the school is not only orderly but equitably focused on academic goals and oriented to continuous improvement. Leaders must also partner with families and communities to ensure that the learning environments outside the school's walls are similarly supportive.

In this chapter you will be asked to consider the role of the school leader in identifying and encouraging effective teaching practice in the classroom, in working with individuals and groups of teachers to effectively implement mandated curricular changes, and in bringing school personnel and families together in collaborative efforts to support student success. You will want to reexamine your own supervisory platform as you explore the challenges associated with providing quality educational experiences for all students.

BEST PRACTICES IN TEACHING

Problem 13: The Ditto Man—A Teacher Who Doesn't Teach

You are a new assistant principal. Your principal has delegated the supervision and evaluation of several teachers to you. You begin to informally visit and observe classrooms.

After visiting Mr. Sabha's classroom several times, you are concerned. Mr. Sabha has been teaching for eighteen years. He teaches science by distributing a packet of handouts. He asks the students to complete the handouts individually. He demands absolute silence in his class and does not allow the students to ask questions. When a student talks, Mr. Sabha writes a discipline referral and sends the student to the office. You have also noticed that Mr. Sabha writes more discipline referrals than do most other teachers.

Today Mr. Sabha wrote a discipline referral on Terry Stewart, a good student who has never had a discipline referral. Terry received a discipline referral for talking. Terry is very upset and is crying.

Case Questions

1. What will you do with Terry?
2. Will you contact Terry's parents or guardians? What will you say?
3. What will you say, if anything, to Mr. Sabha at this point?
4. Will you communicate your concerns about Mr. Sabha to your principal? What will you say?

Suggested Activity

Review the research literature related to supervisory models (clinical, developmental, cognitive, peer coaching). Select what you believe to be the most appropriate model for working with the teacher in this scenario. Explain how you would implement the model with this teacher.

Problem 14: "No Mistakes" Mel—
A Teacher with Unreasonable Grading Expectations

You are a middle school principal. You have a current opening for a seventh-grade social studies teacher. You receive a phone call from the superintendent. The superintendent asks you to accept Mel Valor, a teacher from another school, as a transfer for your position. The superintendent tells you that Mr. Valor's position was phased out at another school and that he needs a new placement. Mr. Valor has a degree, and he has experience in secondary social studies. You agree to accept Mr. Valor's transfer.

Mr. Valor's transition through the preplanning period is uneventful. Once the students begin attending school, problems arise. Several students complain to you that Mr. Valor gives a geography test every Friday. The students are expected to memorize the names and locations of several countries. According to the students, if they misspell or miss one item on the test, Mr. Valor gives them an F.

You meet with Mr. Valor and inquire about his grading policy. He concurs with what the students said. He says that students either earn an A or an F in his class. He further states that there is nothing that you, the students, or their parents can do, because his grading policy is protected under academic freedom.

Case Questions

1. How do you respond to Mr. Valor?
2. How will you investigate his assertions of academic freedom?
3. While you are investigating and formulating a plan, what will you tell students and their parents?
4. At what point, if ever, will you make the superintendent aware of the problems with Mr. Valor?

Suggested Activity

Support or refute Mr. Valor's point of view based on research; applied theory; or federal, state, or district statutes and policies concerning the delivering and assessment of instruction.

Problem 15: The Junkyard Dog—A Teacher Hire Who Is Loyal but Needs Some Finessing in the Area of Curriculum

You are a principal. Your school has two self-contained emotionally handicapped units. One of the classes has had the same excellent teacher for several years. The other classroom has had teacher turnover each year for the past three years. The students have banded together and have been quite difficult for each new teacher.

When you interview Loretta Lowell for the challenging class, you are immediately struck by her honesty and assertiveness. Your guidance counselor and the other teacher of the emotionally handicapped unit also interview Ms. Lowell. They recommend that you hire her. When you check her references, her former principals state that she is an excellent motivator and has strong classroom management skills. You offer Ms. Lowell the position, and she accepts.

During the first few weeks with the students, Ms. Lowell is able to make noticeable differences in the behaviors of her students. You are impressed by her initiative. She touches base with you weekly to let you know of her progress. She not only forewarns you when her children are having bad days but modifies their schedules to minimize emotional outbursts. She communicates well with her students' parents and puts you on alert when one of her students' parents is upset. Ms. Lowell works well with the other teachers. Ms. Lowell honestly communicates with you when other teachers are the roots of some of her children's problems. When you observe Ms. Lowell, her classroom management and interpersonal skills are stellar. You notice, however, that when she presents a lesson, it does not seem to have any organization. For example, you watch her teach a math lesson on fractions, and she rambles about where kids see fractions in real life. When you ask to see her lesson plans, you see that they have one-word titles such as *fractions*. You are concerned that she may not know how to write and organize a lesson.

Case Questions

1. What observation instruments or tools would be most helpful to more clearly diagnose Ms. Lowell's curricular troubles?
2. What lesson plan format could you offer Ms. Lowell that could help her without overwhelming her?
3. If Ms. Lowell asks for feedback on how she is doing, what would you say to her?
4. Besides you, who else could be a helpful resource for Ms. Lowell?

Suggested Activity

Create an action plan that you would use to assist Ms. Lowell in the area of curriculum and instruction.

Problem 16: Circle of Friends—
The Parent of a Disabled Child Who Pushes Too Hard

As grade-level administrator in a large middle school, you have become familiar with many students but have spent substantially more time addressing concerns related to Sam than to those involving any other student. Sam is not a discipline problem. Other than the fact that he is too generous with his hugs and tries to eat french fries off the cafeteria floor, you can usually count on Sam with the help of his protective friends to keep his behaviors within the rules. He is well liked by his peers, and they help him negotiate the crowded hallways, open his locker, and get to class on time. All the same, you have a note on your calendar marking an afternoon appointment with the team of Sam's academic teachers. This is the sixth meeting of the month.

Sam is a special needs student with an actively involved parent. His mother specifically selected your school for her son because of your philosophy of inclusion of special needs students in regular classrooms. Sam is a student with Down's syndrome whose cognitive functioning is at approximately a first-grade level. His individual education plan (IEP) for his sixth-grade year was developed by a team including your predecessor, the teachers and administrators from his elementary school, his mother, and an advocate from a local inclusion support network. Sam's mother was particularly adamant that he be placed in classes with his "circle of friends" to address his social development needs. This circle includes three boys who are placed in a class that contains a cluster of students identified as gifted, a model intended to facilitate the teachers' efforts to differentiate and sometimes accelerate instruction to meet their needs within the regular curriculum. Consequently, despite the functional skills and knowledge identified in the goals in Sam's IEP, he is placed in this advanced-level class. He has a full-time instructional assistant assigned to him, but the level of curriculum modification required to make any of the regular curriculum accessible to Sam is extreme, and additional curriculum must be written by his teachers on a daily basis to address the academic goals of his IEP while including him in class activities that address the regular curriculum.

Sam's mother demands that the teachers meet with her on a weekly basis to involve her in planning for his instruction, and she expects a page-long written description of Sam's progress after each class, frequent phone calls, and additional homework assignments. Sam's mother has been particularly critical of the teachers' efforts to meet his needs within the accelerated class setting and has demanded that her consultant be afforded access to each class to evaluate the teachers' use of content modification and instructional strategies to meet his needs. These extraordinarily dedicated teachers are concerned about the appropriateness of Sam's placement, their ability to effectively meet Sam's needs as well as those of the other thirty students in each class, and what they perceive to be the weekly browbeatings they suffer at the hands of a parent who at times appears to have unrealistic expectations for teachers charged with ensuring the academic success of all 150 students on their multidisciplinary team. They are particularly frustrated with what they perceive as a lack of support and involvement from the special education teacher assigned as Sam's case manager. He has provided few suggestions and no materials to assist the teachers in making modifications or accommodations, and he frequently absences himself from the meetings with Sam's mother. Despite the fact that he is responsible for coordinating the implementation of the IEP, making regular progress reports, and coordinating meetings, these responsibilities have largely fallen upon the shoulders of the other teachers.

As you prepare for your meeting with the teachers, you must consider your ethical and legal responsibilities with regard to Sam and his IEP and to your charge to support the teachers under your guidance and help them address the instructional needs of all of their students. What can you do to work with the teachers, particularly the special education case manager, to effect a favorable outcome?

Case Questions

1. What are the critical issues raised by this scenario?
2. What are the legal and ethical requirements posed by Sam's current IEP?
3. What are the processes that should be followed in addressing this situation?
4. Must the teachers submit to an evaluation of their teaching by the parent's outside consultant?

5. What are the content area teachers' responsibilities?
6. What are the case manager's responsibilities?
7. What are your responsibilities?
8. What would be a positive outcome of your meeting with the teachers?

Suggested Activities

1. Interview a special or exceptional education case worker or resource teacher about the legal and ethical implications of the administrator's role in forming, implementing, and assessing IEPs.
2. Review your school district's policies and procedures that guide administrators' work with the IEP processes.
3. Create a resource handbook for a regular education teacher or for an administrator that addresses the critical information and processes they must have and resources they must know about to support the successful implementation of student IEPs.

**Problem 17: Can't We All Get Along and
Do What We're Supposed to Be Doing?
Troubles between Teachers in an Inclusion Classroom**

You have three inclusion classrooms in grades 1–4. During the second month of school, you start getting complaints from one of the inclusion classrooms. The special education teacher, Sue, and the regular education teacher, Regina, have been working together for the past two years. Their classroom consists of eighteen regular education students and six students with special education eligibility determinations.

Sue comes storming into your office in tears of anger. You seek to understand the problem and allow Sue to talk. Sue explains that Regina does not follow the IEPs for the special education students and has openly criticized the whole concept of inclusion. Sue explains that she has been covering for Regina's unacceptable behavior for the past two years. You ask Sue for specific details about the unacceptable behaviors, but she is reluctant to tell you much more.

You investigate the IEPs of the special education students assigned to Sue's classroom and discover several areas of concern. First, Regina has never attended an IEP meeting since being transferred into the inclusion situation. Second, Regina has failed to update the IEP student progress reports that the regular education teachers are required to complete at the end of each grading period. Third, Regina has been openly critical of the inclusion concept and has stated that she will not work with those "retards" no matter what anyone says.

You go to the classroom to conduct a drop-in evaluation of the teaching and learning. As you enter the room, you notice that Sue is working with the six special education students at a table in the back of the room, while Regina is working with the other students in groups. Regina's groups are engaged and actively learning about a science project they have been working on for several weeks. Sue is working on reading with her students. Over the next couple of weeks, you continue to conduct drop-in evaluations at various times of the day and never observe Regina working with exceptional student education (ESE) students in the learning environment.

Case Questions

1. How would you handle Sue's complaint initially?
2. Is Sue professionally obligated to give you more details about the situation?
3. Before going to the classroom for the drop-in evaluations, what are some things you might consider?
4. Prepare a strategy that you might use to deal with this problem.
5. What steps will you take to monitor the situation?
6. Is there a chance that Regina's personal and professional behaviors can be changed? Please explain your reasoning.
7. What other educational personnel might you consider bringing in to assist with this unhealthy teaching and learning situation?

Suggested Activities

Using the Interstate School Leaders Licensure Consortium or the Educational Leadership Constituent Council Standards as your frame, select one of the following activities and develop it fully, based on the case information provided.

1. Identify and develop an instructional improvement plan for Regina and Sue that will create a learner-centered classroom culture that incorporates the principles of inclusion in teaching and learning.
2. Identify significant other educational personnel who can help support various teaching strategies and desired student outcomes that could help resolve the problems faced in this particular classroom.

Problem 18: Helping Dinosaurs Keep Pace— Instructional Improvement and Change in an Era of Accountability

As a new assistant principal in an urban elementary school whose students have once again failed to make adequate yearly progress as defined by No Child Left Behind, you have been directed to provide in-service to your faculty to facilitate the implementation of the rigid districtwide pacing guides. The curriculum guides provide specific content, suggested activities, and a detailed calendar to ensure that all tested curriculum is taught before the testing in early spring. It is an ambitious, aggressive time schedule that allows for little flexibility and almost no deviation. Your staff, composed largely of veteran teachers, prides itself on knowing what is "important" to teach, and for years the principal has allowed them to make those decisions with little guidance and no interference. Their notions of critical concepts and content do not always correspond to the state and district curricula. Accordingly, you have heard that dinosaur units are taught by teachers at almost every grade, despite the fact that they do not represent content tested in the statewide assessment system. The teachers argue that the needs of their students as they define them supersede the needs of the district and state to have a uniform curriculum. They dismiss the dismal performance of students on the test to the socioeconomic background of their children and a lack of parental support. You have already heard the grumbling about the upcoming staff development day for which you are responsible. Resistance is mounting, and you are likely to face a hostile crowd.

Case Questions

1. What will your staff development plan look like?
2. What might be some of the most critical barriers to success?
3. What strategies might you use with the faculty to ensure that the pacing guides are implemented?
4. What administrative support might the teachers need to implement the guides?
5. How will you monitor and assess the implementation of the pacing guides?

Suggested Activity

Talk with building-level administrators and district-level curriculum supervisors about the processes and challenges involved in curriculum implementation and change. Develop a notebook of strategies and activities that might be used to support teachers in developing curriculum, assessing it, and making needed change.

REFLECTIVE QUESTIONS

1. Describe what you believe to be the best approach to developing curriculum.
2. What research or theory is your approach based on?
3. What are your fundamental beliefs about student learning?
4. Describe your leadership style, and explain how your style will affect curriculum implementation.
5. What are your leadership strengths and weaknesses when attempting to influence curricular change among faculty and staff?
6. How do you or would you determine the professional development needs of your faculty and staff?
7. What do you believe are the best ways to meet the professional development needs of your faculty and staff?
8. What do you need to do to improve your abilities as an instructional leader?

CHAPTER 4

Professional Development and Human Resources

Educational Leadership Constituent Council Standard 4—Professional Development and Human Resources specifies that candidates who complete the program work with faculty and other stakeholders for professional development needs; apply effective supervisory techniques; and identify and apply appropriate policies for recruitment, selection, induction, compensation, and separation of personnel with attention to issues of equity and diversity. Candidates also effectively negotiate and manage collective bargaining issues.

The process of recruiting, developing, and retaining high-performing teachers and staff is critical to the success of every school. And while most state and federal initiatives call for highly qualified teachers in every classroom, their definitions of "qualified" vary wildly. A novice administrator will be challenged by the tasks associated with working with and supporting a diverse group of teachers and staff. Selecting teachers with potential is only half the battle. How we induct new teachers and support their continued professional growth throughout their careers is critical to their success and to student learning. A knowledge of district personnel policies and procedures is essential. But putting student learning at the center of decision making and meeting the needs of teachers and staff who must create the appropriate learning environment and implement an effective instructional program are complex tasks.

Selection and induction of new staff members will undoubtedly be guided by district policy, collective bargaining agreements where they are applicable, and unwritten site-specific traditions that reveal something about the culture of the school. Often the newest and least experienced teachers are given the most challenging assignments, the smallest number of resources, and the greatest numbers of preparations. However, these teachers often consider themselves fortunate to have a classroom to call their own and seldom know whom they can safely turn to for guidance and assistance. Developing purposeful processes for inducting and supporting novice teachers must be a priority. Reflective practice and comprehensive professional growth do not occur by chance. A commitment to continuous improvement and the selection of appropriate strategies to enable individuals and a staff as a whole to develop the capacity to meet student needs is the primary goal of supervision. The effective administrator must be able to use tools in mentoring, coaching, and conferencing to develop and retain effective teachers and staff.

Novice administrators are often asked to supervise employees who are challenging as individuals; who hold sets of values and beliefs that are not consistent with that of the school community; or who lack the knowledge, skills, or will to perform their duties at a high level. To effectively promote a positive school culture that supports student learning, an administrator must understand how to provide leadership that enables faculty and staff to make positive contributions and employ best practice. Whether providing support to a newly hired teacher or helping to reenergize a weary veteran, an administrator must be able to analyze situations, identify needs, and select appropriate strategies. Administrators must take care in making teaching assignments; supervising and evaluating faculty members; and developing an environment where effective instruction, continued learning, and respect are the norms.

In this chapter you will be asked to consider employees in need of assistance and professional development, from the unprepared new teacher to the support staff member who is reluctant to provide the expected leadership necessary to keep operations running smoothly. As you make decisions and select appropriate strategies for resolving conflicts and supporting positive growth, you will be asked to keep your eye on the focal point of schools: ensuring that you are supporting teaching and learning so that all students can learn. Your ability to monitor the culture and climate of a school and to assist all faculty and staff members in applying best practices in their daily work will be critical to your success as an educational leader.

COLLECTIVE BARGAINING

Problem 19: Mr. Confrontation—
A Teacher Who Constantly Asserts Himself

You are an assistant principal. Some of your job responsibilities are to develop and implement guidelines for appropriate student disciplinary procedures and to supervise instructional and noninstructional staff as assigned by the principal. In addition, you are expected to conference with students, teachers, and parents to resolve any problems that affect student learning.

One of the teachers that you have been assigned to supervise is Mr. Proudfoot, a veteran teacher who has fifteen years of experience. He is well respected by the faculty and staff at your school and is seen as a leader. Mr. Proudfoot is the chair of his department. He is also the school representative for the teachers' collective bargaining agency. When you have observed him teaching, you have found that he is an excellent teacher who keeps the students engaged, gets them to think critically, and makes great improvements in the students' comprehension of the content. Mr. Proudfoot has outstanding classroom management skills.

On the other hand, Mr. Proudfoot is confrontational, distrusts the administration, and wants to do things his way. He has confronted you several times.

A student named Robbie Keith was misbehaving in Ms. Singletary's class. Ms. Singletary has poor classroom management skills and does not engage her students well. Mr. Proudfoot asked to have Robbie permanently transferred to his classroom. The other assistant principal and the parents agreed to the transfer, and Robbie has been in Mr. Proudfoot's class for about two weeks. Today, Robbie is sent to your office with a disciplinary referral. This is Robbie's first discipline referral from Mr. Proudfoot; Robbie had two discipline referrals from Ms. Singletary for disrupting class. When you talk with Robbie, he says that

Mr. Proudfoot sent him down because he was not doing his work and was cutting up with some other students. According to Robbie, Mr. Proudfoot said, "I have high expectations academically and behaviorally. If you are going to disrupt the learning environment, then I will see to it that you are suspended out of school."

Mr. Proudfoot finds another teacher to cover his class and comes to talk with you about Robbie. He tells you that Robbie has been misbehaving and not applying himself since he came into Mr. Proudfoot's class. You ask him what he thinks is an appropriate punishment, and he says out-of-school suspension.

You ask if he has contacted or communicated with the parents, and he says no. You are the first administrator to be aware of Robbie's continued disruptions.

Case Questions

1. What documents are you going to review before making a decision? Why?
2. Are you going to speak with anyone (as a resource) before making a decision? If so, who? Why?
3. What type of disciplinary action are you going to assign Robbie for misbehaving in Mr. Proudfoot's class? Why?
4. What will you say to Mr. Proudfoot?
5. What will you say to Robbie's parents?
6. How will your decision and communications affect Mr. Proudfoot's perception that administrators are not to be trusted?
7. How will your decision and communications affect the culture of your school in regard to administrator and union relationship?
8. What proactive steps can you take to improve the relationship that Mr. Proudfoot has with the administration at your school?
9. How should student problems be addressed in Ms. Singletary's class in the future?

Suggested Activities

1. Review your district's collective bargaining agreement. Describe any policies or procedures that are relevant to this case.

2. Write a description that explains how you will support teachers in the area of classroom management. In this description, be sure to include how you will assist in creating student discipline policies for teachers, teams, and departments; review and monitor these discipline policies; and provide assistance for the teachers who are struggling with classroom management.

Problem 20: Beaten "by the Book"— An Assistant Principal Who Did Not Do Her Homework

You are a principal. Your assistant principal, Ms. Benito, has been at your school for one year. You evaluate half of the staff, whereas you have delegated the other half to Ms. Benito. Ms. Benito did well her first year. She listened much and tried to learn the culture of the school. She was a visible presence in the halls of the school and made several informal and formal observations of the teachers.

At the beginning of her second year, Ms. Benito expresses a concern about Ms. Dire, one of the elective teachers who has been teaching for five years. She says that when she observes Ms. Dire, Ms. Dire teaches from her desk. She further states that Ms. Dire lacks enthusiasm and that her lessons frequently do not engage the students. In her class, Ms. Dire typically talks to the students for about five minutes and then distributes a handout for the students to complete individually. You have noticed also that the students' requests for Ms. Dire's course have diminished rapidly in the past three years. You and Ms. Benito concur that Ms. Dire could benefit from some supervisory assistance. Ms. Benito asks if she can work directly with Ms. Dire, and you agree.

When Ms. Benito attempts to assist Ms. Dire, things do not go well. Ms. Dire is greatly offended that anyone would think that she is less than a stellar teacher.

The next time that Ms. Benito observes Ms. Dire, she sees no changes in the instructional pattern. Ms. Benito, with your assistance, prepares for a conference with a written conference summary. This summary notifies Ms. Dire of her less-than-satisfactory performance in the presentation of subject matter. The summary contains a full and complete description of the deficiencies, with corrected suggestions. It also gives a reasonable timeline and an offer for assistance by the administration.

When Ms. Benito attempts to schedule the conference, Ms. Dire happens to miss work for three days due to illness. When Ms. Dire returns, Ms. Benito tries to schedule again. Ms. Dire asks for some time to get caught up from her absences. Ms. Benito, in an effort to truly assist Ms. Dire, agrees. Ms. Benito, however, is then out of the building for two days for in-service training. When they finally are able to meet, two weeks have passed.

Ms. Benito conferences with Ms. Dire and gives her a copy of the conference summary. Ms. Dire is not happy but says very little.

The following day, the union representative notifies you and Ms. Benito that Ms. Dire is filing three grievances against Ms. Benito. The grievances are

1. Ms. Benito did not meet with Ms. Dire within ten days of the observation.
2. Ms. Dire was not given the opportunity for union representation at the meeting.
3. Ms. Dire was not given the opportunity to include her written comments on the conference summary.

Ms. Benito is very upset and feels as though she is in trouble. She reads the union contract and discovers that administrators are to meet with teachers within ten days of making an observation. She also finds that Ms. Dire did not have to be given union representation nor the opportunity to give written comments since this was not a letter of reprimand.

Case Questions

1. What should Ms. Benito have done differently in working with Ms. Dire?
2. How could you as the principal have been a better mentor to Ms. Benito?
3. What do you say to Ms. Benito?
4. How should you respond to the grievances?
5. What actions can you take to ensure a good working relationship with the union representative?

Suggested Activity

Examine a school district's master contract/union agreement. Describe the rights of the employee in this contract that are pertinent to this case study. Then, assume the role of the principal, and write responses to the three grievances described.

PROCESSES FOR SELECTION AND INDUCTION

Problem 21: A Badger in Sheep's Clothing— A Teacher Hire Gone Awry

You are a principal. You are struggling to find a teacher for a self-contained unit of emotionally handicapped students. The class consists of seven boys who are a tough group. They have been in the same class together for years. At times, the boys band together; at other times, they get on each other's nerves because they know each other too well. At least three of the boys have arrest records and have served significant amounts of time in a juvenile detention center for theft and aggravated battery. Almost all of the boys have been diagnosed with learning disabilities, in addition to their emotional disabilities.

Ms. Spaulding is one of two applicants. The other applicant does not have a degree in special education and does not have experience in teaching students with disabilities. Ms. Spaulding has a degree in special education and has taught in that area for three years in another state. Some of her former students were dually placed in her class for the specific learning disabled and the emotionally handicapped. Although you honestly describe what the job entails, Ms. Spaulding says that she really wants to try to make a difference for these students. When you conduct reference checks on Ms. Spaulding, you find that her references are good.

You offer Ms. Spaulding the job and she accepts. You let her know that the behavioral specialist at your school, a former teacher of the emotionally handicapped, has agreed to work with and mentor Ms. Spaulding. On the first day of preplanning, however, Ms. Spaulding is a no-show. You are highly concerned and try to phone her. You are unable to reach her. She finally calls later that day and says that she and her husband were moving over the weekend from out of state. She says that there were problems with her move. She promises that she will be at work the next day.

Ms. Spaulding shows for the second day of preplanning, but she arrives fifteen minutes late to the opening faculty meeting. After the meeting, the behavioral specialist helps Ms. Spaulding create a classroom management system based on the school district's point and level system. Ms. Spaulding seems prepared for the first day of school.

On the first day of school, Ms. Spaulding is a no-show again. The behavior specialist has to cover her class. Ms. Spaulding arrives about thirty minutes after the school starting time. She is dressed inappropriately in a loose tank top that exposes a significant amount of cleavage. The behavior specialist stays with Ms. Spaulding and assists her for the remainder of the day. You decide to conference with her about the pattern of attendance issues that are emerging as well as her dress. She seems to take the information to heart.

On the second day of school, Ms. Spaulding shows and is on time. Her clothes are more appropriate but still questionable. As you are walking by her class, you hear her engage in name-calling with one of her students.

Case Questions

1. What documents are you going to review before setting up another conference with Ms. Spaulding? Why?
2. Are you going to speak with anyone (as a resource) before setting up a conference with Ms. Spaulding? If so, who? Why?
3. What type of disciplinary action, if anything, is warranted for Ms. Spaulding at this point? Please explain.
4. What type of assistance can you provide Ms. Spaulding at this time?
5. In your conference with Ms. Spaulding, what would you say? How would you say it?
6. In the selection process for hiring Ms. Spaulding, what if anything could have been done to avoid the current situation?
7. In the induction process for bringing in Ms. Spaulding, what if anything could have been done better?

Suggested Activity

Describe how a principal should conduct induction programs for teachers who are new to the school. Furthermore, describe how this program should be unique for teachers who teach special education students.

Problem 22: A Lost Lamb— A Teacher Hire from the Business World

You are a middle school assistant principal. Your principal has delegated the task of hiring a teacher for one of your vocational classes, technology. When you advertise the position, you have one applicant, Mr. Gianopolis, who has been an employee for five years in a corporation. At the corporation, he was a professional trainer who taught basic computing skills and software applications to employees. Through the interview and reference checking, you find that Mr. Gianopolis seemed to do well in training adults in the area of technology.

In his personal life, Mr. Gianopolis coached soccer and basketball for the youth leagues in his town. You speak to other coaches and parents about Mr. Gianopolis, and they say that he seems to understand kids and is a natural at working with teenagers.

You also speak to the appropriate person in personnel. You find out that Mr. Gianopolis can be temporarily certified as a public school teacher from the state. Furthermore, you.speak to your principal. You explain what has happened thus far, and your principal recommends that you hire Mr. Gianopolis.

You offer Mr. Gianopolis the position. He accepts. You ask him if he has given any thought to his classroom management plan. He asks, "What's that?"

Case Questions

1. What district resources would be helpful for Mr. Gianopolis?
2. What can you do at the school level to best support Mr. Gianopolis?
3. How can you prevent Mr. Gianopolis from becoming overwhelmed?
4. How often should you touch base with Mr. Gianopolis? Why?

Suggested Activity

Describe how a principal should conduct induction and mentoring programs for new hires who are first-time teachers from the private sector or business world.

Problem 23: Sir, Yes, Sir—A Teacher Who Rules by Intimidation Wants to Be the Technology Specialist

Mr. Rheul—or "Sarge," as the students like to refer to him—is a retired military officer who teaches eighth-grade mathematics with the precision and exacting detail that had been his hallmark on the drill field during his service days. He rules his classroom with a stern demeanor, silencing youthful enthusiasm with a piercing glare and intimidating sarcasm. You and your guidance counselors are kept busy every fall conferencing with parents who object to having their children placed in Mr. Rheul's class. You spend additional time counseling his peers, particularly those who teach on the same interdisciplinary team or serve on school technology committee with him. Sarge is present every day, knowledgeable about his content area, efficient in completing his paperwork, and he works to the letter of his contract. He declared himself head of the math department and considers the technology committee to be his personal fiefdom. He is widely acknowledged as the resident technology expert, and he enjoys building computer systems and advising his colleagues on technology matters. His seeming lack of interpersonal skills and inability to participate appropriately in group activities, however, make him a lightening rod for conflict in an otherwise congenial and collegial school.

You are in the process of working on the initial planning schedule for next year and trying to plan teacher assignments. More than half of the eighth-grade teachers have specifically requested that they not be placed on a team with Sarge, and parents have started making their preemptive calls, trying to save their children from the ninety minutes of lecture that characterize each of his classes. You have had numerous meetings with Mr. Rheul and have sent him to professional workshops to address interactive instructional techniques, student supportive behavior management strategies, and conflict resolution but have seen no visible effects of this targeted professional development. But his students routinely record the highest scores on the state assessments. As you look at the master schedule board, holding Mr. Rheul's request form in your hand, you realize that he has asked for a change in teaching assignment for the coming year.

The school has received a grant to pilot a new technology elective, and the technicians are busy installing a state-of-the-art computer lab, complete with sophisticated graphics and animation software to support the new program. The superintendent has indicated that it is important to get the new program off to a good start because the agency funding the pilot will analyze the result of your school's efforts to determine whether the other middle schools in the district will receive the new labs and software in succeeding years. Mr. Rheul has provided a folder of information, lesson plans, and activities that he intends to implement as part of the new elective course. On paper, it looks good, which is similar to how his lesson plans look. What is your call? Do you keep him in a regular math assignment or move him to the new technology electives position?

Case Questions

1. What are the objectives or guiding principles that will influence your decision?
2. What other information would be helpful to you in making this decision?
3. What alternatives do you have in this situation?
4. What are the potential risks associated with each of the possible courses of action?
5. What are the potential benefits associated with each of the possible courses of action?
6. What factors are most important in making your assignment decisions for Mr. Rheul and for the rest of your staff?
7. What would you do in this situation?
8. What would you do to increase the likelihood that your decision will yield positive results for the students and the school?
9. How would you monitor and assess the extent to which your decision met your objectives?

Suggested Activity

Explore the policies and practices that inform the process of making teacher assignments in your school district and in your school. Interview several administrators about how such decisions are made and what criteria are used.

Problem 24: The Cart before the Horse—The Superintendent Who Hired the Assistant Principal before the Principal

You have just been appointed as the new principal of New Horizon Elementary School. You are eager to get started and have contacted several colleagues that you believe would be strong candidates for the vacant assistant principal's position at New Horizon. Several colleagues indicated that they would like to apply for the position and that they would welcome the opportunity to work with you.

Ms. Parker, the former principal, served there for twenty years, until she was recently elected as superintendent of schools. The superintendent's election was decided by only a few hundred votes. Ms. Parker assumed the superintendent's position midyear.

An interim principal, Mr. Lee, who had no previous administrative experience, was hired to complete the remainder of the school year. Mr. Lee grew up in the community, taught in the middle school of this community, and was well respected in the community. He, too, had applied for the principalship and had strong support from the teaching ranks within the district.

When Ms. Parker realized that the school board members did not consider Mr. Lee as a viable candidate for the principalship, she devised a plan to get him an administrative position. Ms. Parker recommended that the school board hire Mr. Lee as the assistant principal before recommending you as the principal.

The board members had a heated discussion concerning this recommendation. Several argued that the principal should be hired first and that the principal should be allowed to recruit, interview, and recommend his or her own assistant principal to the Board of Education. The school board's decision to hire you over the hometown candidate was determined by a hotly contested three–two vote. You had no idea about the politics of the district until you had already accepted the position.

Case Questions

1. What should you have done before accepting the position?
2. What are some pros and cons of having an assistant principal appointed without your input?
3. How might this politically charged personnel decision affect your supervisory and performance appraisal of Mr. Lee?
4. What are the possible effects of Mr. Lee's appointment on your school's culture? Please explain.
5. What are the likely consequences if you marginalize Mr. Lee's power and authority as your assistant principal?
6. What type of adult learning strategies would you use to mentor and coach Mr. Lee, knowing that he was not the assistant principal of your choice?

Suggested Activities

Using the Interstate School Leaders Licensure Consortium or the Educational Leadership Constituent Council Standards as your frame, select one of the following activities and develop it fully, based on the case information provided.

1. Identify and formulate appropriate policies, criteria, and processes for the recruitment, selection, and induction of new employees that you will recommend to the superintendent to ensure that the likelihood of hiring the assistant principal before the principal does not occur again.
2. Create a plan that will engage Mr. Lee's personal and professional strengths in working with faculty and other stakeholders to identify needs for professional development to organize, facilitate, and evaluate professional development programs.

SUPERVISORY TECHNIQUES

Problem 25: A Sheep in Wolf's Clothing— A Cafeteria Manager Who Dislikes Managing Adults

You are a principal. Ms. McNulty is a new cafeteria manager at your school. She seems to run a tight ship in regard to her budget and in dealing with the students. Ms. McNulty has been outspoken in her dealings with you. She has had an assertive voice when any operation of the school has affected the cafeteria, such as the master schedule, candy sales, and student activity schedules.

As part of her job description, Ms. McNulty's responsibilities include overseeing the cafeteria, the food plan, and cafeteria workers. She is specifically responsible for informing her workers about policy and procedures, and she is responsible for making recommendations to you concerning evaluations and disciplinary actions for her employees.

One afternoon Ms. McNulty comes to see you. She explains that she has two employees who are giving her grief. One of the employees is consistently late to work. The other employee does not get along well with her peers. You ask Ms. McNulty what she has said or done in regard to these issues; she says that she has not done anything. She further states that she would prefer not to do anything. She says that she is not comfortable telling adults what they can or cannot do. She asks that you call in the employees and deal with these matters.

Case Questions

1. What is your responsibility in this situation? What is Ms. McNulty's responsibility in this situation?
2. What are you going to say to Ms. McNulty?
3. How can you support Ms. McNulty?
4. If the problems persist with the employees, how would you treat the two disciplinary issues the same? How would you treat the issues differently?

Suggested Activities

1. Describe how a principal should conduct induction and mentoring for a first-time cafeteria manager.
2. Describe a plan of supervision for cafeteria managers. How often would you meet with them? What would be the objectives or goals? How would you measure their effectiveness?

REFLECTIVE QUESTIONS

1. What core leadership values drive your decisions in human resource planning?
2. Are you an advocate of equal employment opportunity or affirmative action? Please explain.
3. What are some federal and state laws that affect recruitment and selection of employees?
4. What do you feel are the most effective recruitment strategies? How qualified are you as a competent recruiter?
5. What do you think are the most important steps in the selection process? Please explain.
6. What do you believe are your responsibilities as a school leader regarding novice teachers?
7. In your opinion, what are the major purposes of employee performance appraisal?
8. From your perspective, what are the best methods of employee performance appraisal?
9. What procedure does your school district use to establish a salary structure for its employees?
10. What type of relationship do you think should exist between a school leader and a union representative?
11. What are the major issues that are being negotiated in your school district?

CHAPTER 5

Student Personnel Services

Educational Leadership Constituent Council Standard 5—Student Personnel Services specifies that the institution's program prepares school leaders who demonstrate an understanding of, and the capacity to apply, the principles of student growth and development to the learning environment and educational program; who develop with the counseling and teaching staff a full program of student advisement, counseling, and guidance service; who develop and administer policies that provide a safe school environment and promote student health and welfare; who address student and family conditions affecting learning by collaborating with community agencies to integrate health, social, and other services for students; and who plan and manage activity programs to fulfill student developmental, social, cultural, athletic, leadership, and scholastic needs, working with staff, students, families, and community.

Providing for a safe and supportive learning environment is one of the critical tasks challenging the twenty-first-century educational leader. The required knowledge, skills, and dispositions run the gamut from understanding principles of human growth and development to developing active positive connections with families and communities to support student growth. The successful leader must smoothly traverse a landscape framed by a multitude of expectations and needs. Students bring with them a variety of strengths and a seemingly infinite number of needs. Providing the guidance services, positive interactions, intervention programs, and instructional experiences that will enable them to thrive in the school environment are not simple tasks in an era of increased need and diminishing resources. The expectations of families, district and state assessment systems, and the challenges that come with any human endeavor create opportunities for leaders to hone their planning skills as they supervise the instructional and noninstructional staff at the building level.

Teachers bring with them not only knowledge and skills but attitudes that may support or inhibit their efforts to address the needs of the students. Family and community conditions may create situations that challenge the values and assumptions of those charged with helping students meet their academic, developmental, social, and cultural needs. How does an administrator react to situations and conditions that may have been created by the long-standing climate and culture of an institution that may or may not have reflected a sense of valuing of and responsiveness to the students and communities they serve? These challenges are magnified when faced with the actions or inactions of the marginal teacher or noninstructional employee.

The effective administrator must take a proactive stance when planning to meet the needs of all children. One must consider how and when to involve counseling and teaching staff in developing the structures and specialized programs that address student needs in a specific environment. He or she must also consider the context in which the school operates. Each community presents its own set of expectations, values, and issues that must be factored into any plan of action. Developing collaborative relationships with one's internal (faculty, staff, and students) and external (families, community members, district and state officials) publics must be done in ways best calculated to serve the students and promote their success.

In this chapter you will be asked to consider situations in which teachers and a teacher assistant demonstrate a lack of understanding policy. You will encounter a principal who affects the orderly operation of the school with her inconsistent behavior management approach, as well as instructors who, through lack of skill or because of personal issues, fail to provide appropriate supervision and instruction for the students in their care. It is widely believed that an ounce of prevention is worth a pound of cure. As you consider the legal, ethical, and instructional issues in each of the scenarios, consider what proactive practices you might adopt to diminish the likelihood of having to deal with situations similar to those described.

PROMOTING STUDENT HEALTH AND WELFARE

Problem 26: Rigid Roberta—
The Guidance Counselor Who Does Not Bend

Dr. Roberta Smith is the new guidance counselor of the New Hope Charter School. This school is located in a metropolitan area of Florida and is part of a large school district made up of 182 schools. The charter school was created to help children that are one or more grade levels behind in their academic performance. Many of these students have a history of behavioral problems associated with their lack of ability to handle the academic course work at their previous schools.

The New Hope Charter School had more than twenty-seven applicants for the new guidance counselor position. The job advertisement and description clearly outlined the specific challenges that this position would be dealing with. The screening committee narrowed the list of candidates to the top three, who would be interviewed. Dr. Smith was rated the highest because she had her doctorate in childhood counseling and had worked in many school districts in New York. Her reference checks provided no reason to be alarmed. Dr. Smith accepted an invitation for an interview and impressed the search committee with her research and publications in top-tiered journals. Dr. Smith was offered and accepted the job.

During the planning and in-service days before school started, Dr. Smith showed signs that she would be a problem. She built her counseling program on her prior research, cited the findings of her research based on years of working with intercity students in New York, and refused to solicit input from teachers and other professionals on the staff. She refused many of the teachers' and administration's requests to inspect the cumulative records of the students who were enrolled and would start school in a matter of weeks. The tension between the teachers and Dr. Smith began to mount. The teachers went to the principal to complain, and their concerns fell on deaf ears. The administration simply replied that she had the best the credentials and experiences of anyone in the applicant pool and that everyone should give her a chance to prove herself.

As the school opened and the students began classes, Dr. Smith distributed a memo to all teachers that included her counseling schedule.

The memo stated that there would be no deviation from the schedule and that she required all teachers to remain in the class during the large group sessions to manage student conduct. Several teachers approached Dr. Smith, protesting her requirement that teachers stay in the room to manage student conduct. Dr. Smith robustly told the teachers that managing student conduct was the teachers' responsibility and that she was a highly skilled professional that had no time for such tasks. Given the administration's response to earlier complaints, the teachers decided that they would honor the guidance counselor's request and stay in the room during large group counseling sessions.

During the large group sessions that Dr. Smith conducted in various classrooms, teachers witnessed the following:

- Dr. Smith often talked down to the students.
- She used harsh language when talking with students.
- She used highly technical terms that students did not understand.
- She used terms and examples that were not developmentally appropriate for this age group.
- She made negative comments about various community agencies that were providing services for many of the students at this school.
- She made disparaging remarks about the parenting skills of several students' parents in the classroom.
- She would send students out into the hall because they were not paying attention or because they were off task.
- She refused to offer any activities that related to students' social, cultural, and athletic interests. On several occasions she even told the students that these types of programs were a waste of time and that the frills were not part of her interventions.

The teachers met and discussed the concerns and issues that they had witnessed and experienced firsthand. The lead teachers for each grade level agreed to approach Dr. Smith with their concerns and issues in an effort to get her to change. The meeting was a disaster. Dr. Smith berated the teachers and told them that she would never think of telling the teachers how to do their jobs. She told the teachers that if they have any complaints, they should tell the administration. Dr. Smith warned the teachers that telling the administration would be useless because she had full control and autonomy when it came to the counseling arena.

Case Questions

1. List and explain the major principles of student growth and development that this counselor has violated in a short period of time.
2. What are the administrators' responsibilities in this situation? What could they have done better? Please explain your answers.
3. How have the actions of the guidance counselor and administrators affected the concept of a safe school environment and the promotion of student health and welfare? Please elaborate on your answers.
4. What problems might you predict will arise from the parents of the students and the community agencies who work with these students and their families?
5. Were the lead teachers right in approaching Dr. Smith about their concerns? Please defend your answers.

Suggested Activity

Interview an elementary principal, a middle school principal, and a high school principal. Ask them how they develop, with their counseling and teaching staff, student advisement, counseling, and guidance services. Write a summary of your findings.

Problem 27: Underneath It All—An Unstable Teacher

You are an assistant principal. You hire a teacher for learning disabled students. This teacher, Ms. Garcia, is a first-year teacher. Approximately two months into the school year, a shy student, Amanda Miller, who has no history of discipline problems, comes to see you. She says that Ms. Garcia is mean. When you ask her to elaborate, she says that Ms. Garcia screams, yells, and gets hysterical in the classroom. Although you are surprised, you tell the student that you will investigate the situation. In your investigation, you select three students to talk with. Each child confirms what Amanda said about Ms. Garcia. Later that same day, as you are walking a state auditor to the cafeteria, Ms. Garcia rushes up to you. She is sweating profusely and begins to rant and rave in a loud voice in the hallway. Ms. Garcia goes from yelling to crying hysterically saying, "Why are you trying to fire me? Why are you trying to fire me?" Students and teachers are in the hallway going to the cafeteria, too.

Case Questions

1. Do you think that it is appropriate to interview students about Ms. Garcia's reported behavior? Why or why not?
2. If you chose to interview students in your investigation, how would you select the students to interview? Would you interview anyone else besides students?
3. What do you say and do with Ms. Garcia at that moment in the hallway?
4. What do you say to the state auditor?

Suggested Activities

1. Research the options for student counseling at your school. If Ms. Garcia were at your school and had inflicted emotional damage onto students, describe the counseling sessions that you would offer to students. Be sure to include the format (group, individual, pair, etc.), the content (purpose), the duration (how much counseling for how often), and who should counsel.
2. Research your state and district policies on beginning teachers. Describe what the grounds are for dismissal for first-year teachers, and describe what type of support mechanisms (induction programs) are available for first-year teachers.

**Problem 28: Being the New Kid on the Block—
A Novice Assistant Principal**

You are a first-year assistant principal at a middle school. One of your many responsibilities is to develop, implement, and evaluate student attendance policies in accordance with state statute and local school board policy. You have a secretary and a part-time social worker. The social worker comes to your school one day a week.

In addition to an automated phone system that calls the homes of absent students, you and your secretary generate and mail letters to parents of students who miss more than three days in a nine-week period. You also generate and study student attendance data weekly, monthly, and quarterly.

You notice that Louis Fernandez, a seventh-grade student with no history of discipline or absentee problems, has recently been absent quite a bit. He has missed an average of two days per week for the past month. When you investigate, you discover that Louis and his family do not have a phone. You attempt to speak to Louis, but he is absent. You leave a message for the part-time social worker and ask her to make a home visit right away.

One week later, the social worker reports that no one was at the home. You call in Louis and ask him about his absences. At this point, Louis has missed nine days in a nine-week period. Louis says that he has been sick a lot. He also says that he has a five-year-old sister who has been sick a lot, and he explains that when his sister is sick, he has to stay home and take care of her so that his mother can go to work. You tell Louis to ask his mother to come to school tomorrow. He agrees.

The very next day Louis is absent again. You drive to his house. When you arrive, you meet his mother. You explain Louis's attendance problem, and she becomes visibly upset. She begins to cry and speak in Spanish. She says that Louis lied about having to stay home with his sister. She explains that Louis has been hanging around with some older boys and that she feels like she has lost control of him. She says that she wanted to come to school and ask for help, but she did not have a car. She says that she even stopped a policeman who was in her neighborhood and told him that she knew her son was skipping school. She asked the policeman to help her find her son, and, according to Louis's mother, the policeman said, "Lady, we have bigger fish to fry. That's not my job." She begs you to help her with her son.

Case Questions

1. If you do not know how to help this parent, who could you talk to within your school district?

2. When you see Louis again, what are you going to say to him?
3. What are some ways that you can help this parent with her child?
4. How can you regularly communicate with this parent since she does not have a phone or car?
5. What do you think should be done about the comment made by the policeman?

Suggested Activities

1. Create a flow chart that describes intervention activities used in your school or school district to deal with truants.
2. Make a database of all social service agencies in your area that could help parents with truant children. Be sure to include the following information: name of agency, name of contact person, phone numbers, addresses, operating hours, fees, and the type of services provided.

Problem 29: Kaboom! A Science Teacher Who Is Incompetent

Ms. Olive, a veteran teacher who began her career as a home economics teacher, has for the last seven years been teaching seventh-grade life science. An investigation into the source of a previous explosion in her science lab was inconclusive in terms of causation, but it is well known throughout the school community that she has significant issues with classroom management. While her classroom observations have been marginal, she has, under the current and previous three administrations, received satisfactory evaluations. The previous assistant principal was reassigned after the teacher and the teachers' union suggested that the less-than-satisfactory evaluations given by that administrator were racially motivated. New observations were conducted by another administrator, and Ms. Olive received a satisfactory performance rating in her final evaluation for that year.

As a new assistant principal, you have been called to her classroom to restore order on numerous occasions; as well, students and parents have raised concerns regarding students playing with gas jets during class lectures and receiving inaccurate content information. The guidance counselor is concerned because an increasing number of parents are refusing to have their students in this teacher's class, creating significant challenges in following district class size regulations, causing perceptions of differential treatment of students, and raising concerns for those who remain in the biology sections she teaches.

Ms. Olive has been assigned to you for evaluation purposes. During your first observation of Ms. Olive, you note that her lesson includes having students watch a movie about whales despite the fact that the learning standards being addressed have to do with fish. You witness a student playing games on his cell phone, and a scuffle breaks out as students move from one activity to the next. Throughout the class, an unphased Ms. Olive calmly remained seated behind her desk.

Case Questions

1. What issues will you address with Ms. Olive in your postobservation conference?
2. What documentation will you gather to illustrate your concerns about Ms. Olive's instruction and class management?
3. What will you discuss with your principal?
4. How will you respond to parent concerns regarding Ms. Olive?

Suggested Activity

Review your school district's policies for supervising instructional personnel. Write a memorandum to your principal, outlining the steps that you recommend for dealing with this teacher in regard to ensuring a safe school environment that promotes student health and welfare and monitoring the curriculum within her classroom.

Problem 30: I Don't Have Time to Do That!
A Teacher Assistant with a Bad Attitude

You are the assistant principal at New Horizon Elementary School. Latoya Williams just transferred to New Horizon from a small rural school in Kentucky. Her cumulative school records indicate that she was in the fifth grade at her former school and has been socially promoted three times in her academic career. Latoya's legal guardian is now her grandmother, Ms. Lee.

Additional information found in her file indicates that she has been in and out of six different schools during the past two years. One month later, the special education coordinator at New Horizon realizes that Latoya is eligible for special services. You convene a meeting with the school's child study team to develop an individual education plan to meet Latoya's educational needs. Within two weeks, the child study team has reached consensus on the plan. You schedule a meeting with the regular education teachers, the special education teachers, all of the fifth-grade teacher assistants, the school counselor, Latoya, and her grandmother to discuss the plan.

In short, the child study team has determined that Latoya should be placed in Ms. Ballard's fifth-grade class because Ms. Ballard is certified in special education, is an excellent teacher, and loves working with some of the neediest children in the school. In addition, Ms. Ballard has six fewer students than do the other fifth-grade teachers and has a full-time teacher assistant in her class at all times. When this decision is made, Ms. Ballard is pleased and warmly invites Latoya and Ms. Lee to the classroom for a personal visit.

Pleasantries are exchanged among the child study team, Latoya, and her grandmother. Just before everyone starts to get up from the table and depart the meeting, things take a turn for the worst. Ms. Rudd, Ms. Ballard's teacher assistant, slams her notebook on the table and loudly states, "I don't have time to do all the documentation and paper work for a child that is so far behind in school. I'll never be able to catch her up to grade level. This is ridiculous!"

Case Questions

1. As the assistant principal and member of the committee to help special education students, what do you say and do when Ms. Rudd acts inappropriately at the close of the meeting?
2. Does Ms. Rudd's behavior warrant punishment? If so, what type of punishment would be in order?
3. What conversations would you have with Ms. Ballard concerning Ms. Rudd's employment history before making a decision about Ms. Rudd?

4. Do you believe that Latoya's placement in Ms. Ballard's room is appropriate to promote the student's health and welfare? Please explain your answer.

5. How can you apply the principles of student growth and development and attempt to manage teachers who may have this type of disposition?

6. What affect might Ms. Rudd's behavior have on the learning environment and the educational programs at your school?

Suggested Activities

Using the Interstate School Leaders Licensure Consortium or the Educational Leadership Constituent Council Standards as your frame, select one of the following activities and develop it fully, based on the case information provided.

1. By collaborating with community agencies and other educational personnel, develop a workshop that can be delivered to school employees that stresses the principles of student growth and development and that addresses student and family conditions affecting student learning.

2. Formulate a team of educational personnel that can help employees who are under a great deal of stress and frustration. Describe who would be on the team and describe what strengths they have to help a stressed employee deal with policies related to promoting student health and welfare.

3. With the counseling and teaching staff, create a presentation that you can use as a staff development program for compliance issues for the district and the school as related to students who are in special education programs.

Problem 31: Vacillating Vivian—A New Principal Who Lacks Consistency in School Discipline

You are an assistant principal at a school. You have been at the school for seven years. The school is located in a neighborhood where

80 percent of the students are on free and reduced lunch. The ethnic background of the school population is 35 percent African American, 35 percent Hispanic, 25 percent Caucasian, and 5 percent Vietnamese. The former principal, Mr. Blake, had been at the school for fifteen years; he hired you. Mr. Blake was a firm but fair disciplinarian. He was a kind man who ran a tight ship. Under his leadership, the school ran smoothly with few major disciplinary issues. Mr. Blake retired, and Ms. Vivian Vargus was hired as the new principal. Ms. Vargus was an assistant principal for five years at another school.

Under Ms. Vargus's leadership, things are quite different. Students are openly disrespectful to her and teachers, and she shrugs it off as "the students are just having a bad day." Teachers complain that they will not send students to see Ms. Vargus for disciplinary infractions because she talks with them, gives them candy, and sends them back to class. When you come down hard on students for major infractions such as fighting, the students appeal to Ms. Vargus, who reverses your decision. Lately you have noticed an increase in the number of student fights among ethnic groups. You are concerned that things are escalating to the point of a possible riot.

Case Questions

1. What, if anything, do you say to Ms. Vargus?
2. Should you go to someone above Ms. Vargus and discuss these issues? If so, who? What would you say?
3. What do you say to the complaining teachers?

Suggested Activity

Create a template for schoolwide discipline. Describe the components that would be part of the plan.

REFLECTIVE QUESTIONS

1. How can you as a school leader meet the diverse student needs (developmental, social, cultural, athletic, leadership, and scholas-

tic needs), particularly those students representing different cultural groups?

2. What do you believe are the keys to understanding and dealing with a student who has a disability?

3. What federal and state statutes do you use to guide your decisions regarding exceptional student education?

4. When a student has discipline problems, what are the most positive interventions to use?

5. What do you believe are the major causes of violence in schools today?

6. What should be the primary goals of all extracurricular activities?

7. What strategies are most effective in forming partnerships with parents?

8. Do you agree with the following statement? "Schools and school districts are the key coordinators for the network of services available to children." Please explain.

9. What types of community partnerships are readily available in your school district? What types of community partnerships need to be developed?

10. What do you believe are the major functions of school psychologists?

11. What are the major roles that school guidance counselors should fulfill?

12. How can you as an educational leader maintain the balance between the students' needs and development and the pressure for academic accountability?

CHAPTER 6

Organizational Management

Educational Leadership Constituent Council Standard 6—Organizational Management specifies that candidates who complete the program are educational leaders who have the knowledge and ability to promote the success of all students by managing the organization, operations, and resources in a way that promotes a safe, efficient, and effective learning environment.

A primary responsibility of the educational administrator is to develop the knowledge, skills, and requisite capacities to manage his or her organization; coordinate its operations; and act as a good steward of its resources in a way that supports the development of a safe, efficient, and effective learning environment. Managing an educational organization requires a versatile set of strategies and a systems view of organizational structures, behaviors, and communications.

For more than fifty years, organizational theorists have examined the impact that the behaviors of people have on organizations. They have examined issues of leadership, conflict resolution, and decision making on the very structures of the organizations and the core values that underpin them. As we have come to understand schools as open systems—organizations that operate not in a vacuum but as organic interactive entities that are influenced by internal and external constituencies—it has become clear that among the skill sets that an effective school leader must demonstrate is the ability to develop and monitor effective group processes that build a capacity for effecting and sustaining change and achieving organizational goals.

While there are numerous models for the processes of leading organizations, creating and sustaining strategic change, and building organizational structures that are responsive to the environments in which they operate, how does one choose the appropriate models? How does a leader determine what strategies are most appropriate in a given situation? How does one determine how, when, and to whom to delegate authority and responsibility?

In the final analysis, one of the most critical factors in the success or failure of the implementation of any strategy or the adoption of any set of processes is the people who must embrace and implement the plans. The instructional and noninstructional staff must have clear notions of their roles and responsibilities, share a common sense of purpose, and have the will and the capacity to work together to realize the mission and vision of the school community. When roles or functions are not clearly defined or when individuals fail to perform at the expected levels, the administrator as supervisor and manager of the school must be prepared to respond, understanding that every choice and every action may have ripple effects throughout the organization.

In this chapter you will be asked to consider several scenarios that call for you to exercise critical thinking and decision-making skills that demonstrate an awareness of the big picture. As you react to the situations presented, we invite you to consider how various theoretical models inform the ways in which you might take a proactive stance to establish operational plans that help your school accomplish strategic goals. In addition, you may want to consider how you will delegate responsibilities and authority effectively and how you will continually monitor and assess the progress that your faculty and staff make toward attaining their common goals. Most important, you must think about the potential intended and unintended consequences of the actions you choose in response to each situation and how they might affect the school as a whole.

After responding to each case study and engaging in the suggested activities, revisit the personal platform statement on ethical leadership behavior that will guide you in your decision making and actions, and revise it to include the principles of organizational management that will be your hallmark as an educational leader.

DEFINITION OF ROLES

Problem 32: But She Makes Great Coffee—
The Incompetent Secretary

You are an assistant principal new to your high school. Before your appointment, the former assistant principal hired a secretary for the assistant principal's office. The former assistant principal hired someone who could "take care of him" and who had good people skills for working with parents and students. As time progresses, you discover that the job responsibilities for the secretarial position include typing reports and letters on the computer, keeping an effective filing system for the assistant principal's office and personal files, compiling data with your supervision, and taking and transcribing dictation. You also learn that the current secretary has the ability to type about fifteen words per minute, has difficulty using the computer, does not know how to dictate or transcribe, and may not be functionally literate. She does, however, have good people skills and is willing to learn. Several teachers like the secretary and socialize with her. Other teachers complain about the secretary, saying that they are embarrassed by her incompetence.

Case Questions

1. Describe the professional relationship that assistant principals should have with their secretaries.
2. How could your principal be supportive in this situation?
3. What do you say to those teachers who complain to you about the secretary's incompetence?
4. What are the emotional consequences of this situation on the secretary, the teachers who like her, the teachers who are embarrassed by her, and you?

Suggested Activity

Review your school district's policies for supervising noninstructional personnel. Create an intervention plan for the secretary. Describe strategies and a timeline that you would use to work with the secretary.

Problem 33: Lazy Larry—A Custodian Who Doesn't Clean

Note: The following case study was submitted by graduate student Troy Krotz and edited by Dr. Robert Egley.

Assume that you are an assistant principal at a high school of approximately twenty-two hundred students. One of your responsibilities is that of plant operations, and you are responsible for supervising all of the custodial staff. One of the custodians, Larry Gray, has received several complaints concerning his work performance for several years. He has been part of the night crew for twenty-two years, which is longer than any other custodial staff member. He has been responsible for cleaning the classrooms and restrooms in building 1, which houses the English department and some special education classes. County guidelines call for all classrooms to be vacuumed, chalkboards to be washed, chalk trays to be cleaned, and the garbage to be emptied on a nightly basis. Most teachers are just happy to have their garbage emptied nightly and the other jobs done every two or three days.

Ms. Green, the English department chairperson, comes into your office and tells you that she wants to lodge another complaint against Larry. She tells you that she has tried to be patient but that Larry has not vacuumed her room in two weeks and has not cleaned the chalk trays or washed the board in six days. She tells you that the rest of building 1 is complaining to her, and she demands that either Larry get his act together or you come clean her room. You assure Ms. Green that you will look into the matter, and you wish her a good day.

After returning from lunch duty, you see Ms. Gordon heading toward your office. She also teaches in building 1 and appears to be very angry. She tells you that she has had enough of Larry and her filthy room. Over the past six weeks, she has kept a close eye on two french fries that have been sitting on her floor behind the trash can. She tells you that she has deliberately left them there to see if Larry would do his job properly and pick them up. It has now been six weeks, and she tells you that the french fries are moldy and that the mold has started to spread on the carpet. She demands that something be done about Larry since she has made several complaints about him over the past four years.

At the end of the day Larry comes in early to meet with you. He starts the meeting by telling you he has been at this school for twenty-two years and has gone through four principals and has worked under seven assistant principals. You try to keep the meeting focused and tell Larry that there have been several complaints about the way building 1 is being cleaned. There are concerns that he is not completing the required tasks each night. He tells you that he has been very busy and has had to pull double duty on several occasions because of the other night crew members calling in sick. You try to be sympathetic but tell him that he still must clean each room nightly according to the county guidelines. He tells you he will try harder but that he can only get so much done in one night.

Over the next two weeks, everything is great in building 1. When you see Ms. Green and Ms. Gordon in the hall, you ask them how things have been, and they tell you that things are fine. After four weeks, Ms. Green is back in your office because her room has not been vacuumed, again, for two weeks and several members of her department have again come to her with complaints about their rooms. Ms. Green again demands that something be done.

Case Questions

1. What do you do now?
2. How do you deal with the teachers in building 1 who keep getting upset every time Larry gets lazy about doing his job properly?
3. Does Larry's work performance warrant further action from the administration? If yes, what would the next steps be?
4. What are the likely consequences if you move Larry to another building?
5. How important is it for you to handle this situation to its conclusion knowing how the staff feel about the administration?

Suggested Activities

Using a systems perspective to the job performance problems of Larry, viewing schools as interactive internal systems operating with external partnerships within the school, select one of the following aspects and develop it fully, based on the case information provided:

1. Establish operational plans and processes to accomplish your desired goals and objectives to improve Larry's job performance.

2. Discuss and explain the appropriate communication strategies you might use to resolve the job performance problems in Larry's case.
3. Formulate how you plan to monitor and assess the progress of Larry's job performance. Be sure to include adjustments and the formulation of new action steps, as may be necessary.
4. Develop an efficient budget-planning process that is driven by district and school priorities and involves staff and community related to the workload distribution when custodial staff members are absent.

Problem 34: What's My Job?
Unclear Roles or Ineffective Teacher Assistants

Note: The following case study was submitted by graduate students Alicia Riggs and Ellen Spencer and edited by Dr. Robert Egley.

Assume that you are a new principal at a large elementary school with fifteen hundred students in grades K–5. You have two assistant principals. One is experienced with facilities and new construction of schools, so you have assigned her to this yearlong project. The other assistant principal has extensive experience leading the fourth and fifth grades, so you have assigned him to oversee these grade levels. You have decided to be the instructional leader of the lower elementary grades K–3.

The lower grades have low student-to-teacher ratios because you have recently received large federal dollars to support such an instructional model. The lower elementary grades have ten to twelve teachers per grade level. Each teacher has a teacher assistant. Because of the large instructional staffs in the lower grades, you have decided to appoint "lead teachers" to help you with the instructional demands of large student enrollment, new construction, and the day-to-day logistical operations of this large school. You supported the concept of having them attend all specials, such as art, music, physical education, and computer labs with the students. This would allow the grade-level teachers time to meet with the lead teacher to discuss the educational needs and progress.

When you meet with your lead teachers during the second week of school, you realize that there is a problem between the lower elementary teachers and their teacher assistants. Your lead teachers inform you of the following problems with the teacher assistants:

- They are not complying with their duty to attend specials with the students.
- Some have failed to complete instructional tasks assigned to them by their supervising teachers.
- Some are not staying with the students during the entire lunch period.
- Many are constantly out of the classroom during instructional time.

The lead teachers ask you if it is your job as principal to address this problem or if they should deal with the problem at their level?

Case Questions

1. Is it your responsibility to speak to the teacher assistants first?
2. What is your immediate response to the lead teachers?
3. Would the development of a job description be helpful? If so, who should be involved in the process? Why?
4. How much time should be given to resolve the problems associated with this situation?
5. Who is ultimately responsible for the behavior of the teacher assistants in this case?
6. Describe some possible effects or outcomes if one or more of the teacher assistants is reassigned, removed, or replaced.

Suggested Activity

Use the Interstate School Leaders Licensure Consortium or the Educational Leadership Constituent Council Standards as your frame. Develop a long-term plan for monitoring the working relationships between the teachers and the teacher assistants that will help ensure the smooth and efficient delivery of instruction. Explain the various management techniques and group processes you will use to define roles, assign functions, delegate effectively, and determine accountability for attaining goals and objectives related to the case.

MONITORING AND ASSESSING PROGRAM ACTIVITY AND GROUP PROCESSES

Problem 35: But That's How They Voted—
Process without Purpose for a Struggling New Principal

Bob Newley is in the second year of his principalship in a large middle school in a metropolitan area. His first year at the helm of Progress Middle School was marked by significant discipline issues, lagging student achievement (as measured by the state assessment system), and low staff morale (as evidenced by the 56 percent of the instructional staff who requested transfers to other schools at the end of the year). In an effort to provide support for this struggling novice administrator, the school district administration has assigned you to serve as a mentor for Bob and to help him develop effective organizational management skills.

In your first meeting with Principal Newley, you ask him to identify what he sees as significant challenges for the new year. He indicates that he was most concerned with getting the staff to "quit grumbling all the time" and take on some responsibilities around the school. He is having trouble getting teachers to come forward to fill key leadership roles, something that he attributes to a lack of professionalism. When pressed for specific examples that illustrate the issue, Bob relates the story of one of his dissatisfied teachers.

His assistant principal has come to him and indicated that one of the English teachers is unhappy and already talking about requesting a transfer. She is one of two returning teachers in the department of ten, and she is the one who has demonstrated the greatest leadership at the department, grade, and school levels. At issue, according to the assistant principal, is the dissatisfaction that the teacher had expressed about "how things are done around here."

Just before the end of the previous school year, Bob had sent Ms. Kate Acton, a young but capable teacher, a memo changing her assignment for the current year. She had been working with a special program addressing the needs of at-risk students, but the department head, a teacher with seniority, had requested this dropout-prevention position; so, on that basis, Bob had moved Ms. Acton to a different assignment at the same grade level within the department. After the department head left, taking an administrative position at another school during the third week of the new school year, Bob asked Kate if she would be willing to assume the role of department head, and he offered her an opportunity to return to the vacated teaching assignment. She declined the reassignment and asked for an evening to consider the offer of the leadership position.

In the meantime, one of the assistant principals indicated that there was another teacher, a first-year alternative certification teacher, who had expressed interest in the job and advised that it would be most fair to have an election. Bob immediately had his secretary e-mail a memo announcing the election, listing the two teachers' names. Apparently Ms. Acton, according to the assistant principal, was not only taken aback by the change in plans but was disheartened when the provisionally certified teacher won the election and Kate was asked to train her so that the assessment monitoring and other responsibilities could still be accomplished. When Bob tried to placate her by having the assistant principal offer her an opportunity to be trained as a mentor, Ms. Acton wryly pointed out that it would be one of her responsibilities to mentor her new department head and said that she did not think that would be appropriate. She declined to become a mentor, and Bob has the impression that she has shared her dissatisfaction with her colleagues, something that he believes contributes to their unwillingness to participate in committee work and take on responsibilities beyond their own classrooms. The English department is floundering under the guidance of the newly elected head without the help of Ms. Acton and the other experienced teacher; the early assessment data reports have not been generated; and the curriculum pacing guides he asked for have not been completed. What, Bob asks, is he to do with this "bad apple" that is adversely affecting morale at Progress Middle School?

Case Questions

1. How do you respond to Bob?
2. What do you believe to be the most significant issue (or issues) embedded in the situation that Bob has described?
3. Is there anything that you might have advised Bob to consider doing differently?

4. What would you recommend that Bob do at this point in the year?
5. How would you go about working with Bob to help him address the issue he has raised and any that you may have identified?

Suggested Activity

Interview five teachers about their experiences with and preferences regarding communications and processes in their schools. List the key themes that emerge from their responses and compare them to what you have read about organizational management and communication. Identify the critical principles that would guide your efforts to manage group processes in your school setting.

SYSTEMS PERSPECTIVE

Problem 36: Birds of a Feather Who Stick Together— A New Principal Who Seeks Change and a Staff That Rebels

Dr. Jones is the new principal of Monte Vista Middle School, located in a rural area of Florida and part of a large school district made up of 102 schools. Monte Vista employs two assistant principals, Mr. Snow and Ms. Sine, who share the responsibility for the near one thousand sixth-, seventh-, and eighth-grade students. Dr. Jones is a proactive and hands-on principal, making it his business to know what is going on at his school and visiting classes nearly every day of the year.

Ms. Williams has been teaching ESE classes at Monte Vista for ten years and is respected by many staff members for her fair approach with students and her infrequent discipline referrals. Ms. Williams typically instructs specifically learning disability students and this year was relocated to a room in the newly constructed back wing of the campus, somewhat removed from the rest of the school. Ms. Williams has received satisfactory evaluations each year with the exception of last year, when the former principal noted three areas that needed improvement: classroom management, student monitoring, and fulfilling contracted times of arrival to and departure from the school.

Dr. Jones began his year at Monte Vista by reviewing staff files, specifically examining evaluations for the past few years. Dr. Jones consulted his administrative team and gathered names of instructors and support staff who were demonstrating performance that was determined to be of relatively low quality. From the evaluations and administrative team recommendation, Dr. Jones began his improvement observations of five classroom teachers, including Ms. Williams, with the intention of monitoring and implementing improvement plans if needed.

On the first day of Dr. Jones's observations, Ms. Williams arrived five minutes after the bell rang for the second period. As Dr. Jones more closely monitored Ms. Williams and her classroom over the following three days, he discovered that she would come to at least one class late every day. On the third day of his observations, the school resource officer was called to Ms. Williams's room. An investigation revealed that she had allowed three seventh-grade ESE students to leave her room and play football outside on the grass unsupervised. Consequently, the students threw rocks at a car across the street from the school and were videotaped doing so. The students revealed that this was not the first time that Ms. Williams had allowed them to play outside her classroom unsupervised. Upon a third observation, an assistant principal found a fourth-period class to be completely unsupervised. When asked where their teacher was, the students responded that Ms. Williams had left to use the restroom.

Dr. Jones places Ms. Williams on a detailed plan of improvement based on the aforementioned incidents. He handles every aspect of this task according to district policy and the protocol of the professional practices department. He schedules an appointment with Ms. Williams to explain the plan of improvement to her. The two assistant principals, Mr. Snow and Ms. Sine, are included in this official meeting with Ms. Williams. During the meeting, Ms. Williams become furious and walks out of his office and refuses to sign her copy of the document. Within hours, the news has spread throughout the entire school.

Later that day, Mr. Washington, the union representative for the school district, calls Dr. Jones and asks to meet with him concerning his decision to place Ms. Williams on a plan of improvement. Dr. Jones agrees to meet with Mr. Washington after school in his office. Mr. Washington informs Dr. Jones that he might want to schedule the meeting in the auditorium because nearly every teacher at his school plans to attend this meeting in opposition to his actions against Ms. Williams, his leadership style, and his harsh tactics in dealing with veteran teachers.

Case Questions

1. Knowing the problems noted with last year's evaluation of Ms. Williams, was it a good idea to relocate her to a remote part of the campus? Please explain your reasoning.
2. Was Dr. Jones wise to review former evaluations from previous years and to speak to his administrative staff concerning the performance of the instructional personnel? Why or why not?
3. Did Dr. Jones overreact by placing Ms. Williams on a plan of improvement so early in the school year? Please justify your answer.
4. Is interviewing students about teachers a good method for accumulating usable information? What are the pros and cons of this type of information gathering?
5. Is Dr. Jones wise to meet with the union representative? How about meeting with the representative with the teachers present?
6. How would you recommend that Dr. Jones deal with the teachers who indicated that they would attend this meeting?
7. What actions should Dr. Jones take in dealing with Ms. Williams's getting angry, refusing to sign her copy of the plan of improvement, and storming out of his office?
8. What might you have done differently in this case? Why?

Suggested Activity

Identify at least five key leaders who will need to support the actions taken by Dr. Jones for him to survive the fire of this ordeal. Justify why each was selected and identify his or her role in the supporting of Dr. Jones.

OPERATIONAL PLANS AND PROCESSES

Problem 37: The Neighborhood School—
A Principal without a Plan for After-School Supervision

You are an assistant principal who is new to a high school. After bus duty in the afternoons, you notice several groups of students hanging out at the school. Most of the students are talking among themselves while waiting for parents to pick them up or while dawdling before walking home. A few of them engage in horseplay, and no adults are actively supervising the students. As teachers walk around campus running errands, they speak to students who are misbehaving. You are concerned about student safety and liability and speak to your principal about your concerns. Her response is that this is a neighborhood school, and she wants the students to always feel welcome here. She believes that there is no problem. Later, a few teachers voice concerns to you as well in regard to a lack of after-school supervision and to student safety.

Case Questions

1. Should you approach your principal again? What if anything do you say to the principal?
2. Should you go to someone above the principal and discuss these issues? If so, who? What would you say?
3. What do you say to the complaining teachers?
4. Describe the optimum professional relationship that should exist between a principal and his or her assistant principals.

Suggested Activity

Create an after-school supervision plan for high school students. Include in this plan how students who ride the bus, who wait to be picked up by parents, who drive themselves, and who walk home will be supervised. Describe who will supervise the students, how they will be supervised, and for what length of time.

REFLECTIVE QUESTIONS

1. In your opinion, what are the duties of a principal in running an effective school? What are the assistant principal's responsibilities?
2. Why is the principal usually considered the most important individual of any given school?

3. What are some characteristics of highly effective schools?
4. Should a principal be an instructional leader, a school manager, or both? Please explain.
5. Analyze your current school. What are some of the organizational characteristics that make your school challenging for its leader?
6. From your perspective, what are some helpful strategies in working with noninstructional staff?

CHAPTER 7

Interpersonal Relationships

Educational Leadership Constituent Council Standard 7—Interpersonal Relationships states that the institution's program prepares school leaders who demonstrate the capacity to understand and use appropriate interpersonal skills; written, verbal, and nonverbal communication; communication strategies; counseling and mentoring skills; and stress management and conflict management techniques.

Leading is, at its heart, a human endeavor. The success or failure of any organization rests with the people. Teachers and staff members in any school community function individually and collectively at different developmental levels at various stages of their adult and career lives. Their levels of abstraction and commitment affect the work they do and define the level and nature of the supervisory support they require. When one adds to this mixture differing communication styles, as well as varied and sometimes conflicting priorities, and places them in the often pressure-packed environment of a school, many things can happen.

Communications appear to be at the center of most successful and unsuccessful attempts to solve problems and build community in schools. Among the important relationships that set the tone and shape the climate of the school are the relationships between the principal and the teachers. Establishing trust, setting clear goals, and treating faculty members equitably is key to ensuring that the culture of the organization will support student learning. Respect for all school community members is an essential ingredient in conflict management, problem solving, and supervisory practice in general. A good leader not only models appropriate interpersonal relationship skills in his or her daily interactions with faculty, staff, students, and parents and caregivers but fosters those skills in all members of the school community.

In this chapter you will encounter situations that involve breakdowns in communications. From sharp-tongued teachers to well-intentioned administrators, the situations and personalities represented in each scenario provide an opportunity for you to identify behaviors and strategies that you can employ to communicate effectively and respectfully with the members of your school community.

INTERPERSONAL SKILLS

Problem 38: Sharp-Tongued Sharon—
A Teacher Whose Words Hurt Children

You are a high school assistant principal who evaluates several teachers at your school. One of the teachers that you supervise directly is Sharon Blade. Sharon says that she believes in the "old school" way of doing things. She thinks that teenagers should be quiet and respectful. She has a hard time understanding why some students do not come to class prepared with pencil and paper. Sharon writes at least five student discipline referrals a day. Most of the referrals are for menial things, such as talking without permission or not being prepared for class. When dealing with these discipline referrals, the students often tell you that Ms. Blade favors certain students in her class. Students also inform you that when they get on the wrong side of Ms. Blade, she picks on them. Today you were called to Ms. Blades's class to remove a disruptive student, Christine Wiggins. When you arrive at the classroom, Christine is stomping back and forth outside Ms. Blades's door. Christine is talking loudly to herself, calling Ms. Blade a "bitch." Ms. Blade rushes to the door and says in front of Christine and her class, "I do not have to tolerate this. She should act like a young lady. I can't help that she has a miserable home life. She's going to end up like her sister—pregnant at the age of fifteen." With that, Ms. Blade slams her door shut, leaving you and Christine in the hall.

Case Questions

1. How will you de-escalate Christine?
2. How will you deal with Christine's classroom disruption and use of profanity?
3. How will you deal with the inappropriate things that Ms. Blade said about Christine?
4. How will you handle parent complaints about the outbursts from Ms. Blade and Christine?

Suggested Activities

1. Create an intervention plan for Ms. Blade. Describe strategies and a timeline that you would use to work with Ms. Blade so that she can develop better rapport with all of the students in her class.
2. Research the code of ethics in your state and school district. What does the code say in regard to teachers' showing sensitivity; exhibiting respect; showing tact; and promoting multicultural awareness, sensitivity, and appreciation? Describe how the code applies to this scenario.
3. If a student is not getting appropriate supervision and care at home, describe counseling or mentoring programs that are readily available within your school or community.

Problem 39: Cyber-Argument Complication

As an assistant principal in an elementary school, one of your responsibilities is to participate in the development of individualized education plans (IEPs) for students with diagnosed learning disabilities. On Monday morning, you are called away to handle an emergency situation, and another assistant principal takes your place at a meeting with the IEP team for Ray, a student who has been diagnosed with an emotionally handicapping condition. At issue are decisions about the appropriateness of Ray's behavioral intervention plan and the least restrictive environment that constitutes an appropriate placement for him.

As you return to your office at the end of the day, your colleague, the other assistant principal, approaches you and says, "We have to talk."

Apparently, as the teachers shared their input and observation data about Ray's behaviors and responses to the intervention strategies in place, a consistent pattern seemed to be emerging. Each teacher described the ways in which they attempted to implement the IEP and accommodate Ray in their classes, but teacher after teacher described his uncontrolled fits of rage, the continual threats he directed at the teacher and at his peers, and frequent occasions when he appeared to be talking to persons unseen. His academic progress was obviously suffering from his inability to engage in regular class activities. Several of the teachers indicated that they feared for the safety of other students in the class and for Ray's own safety and well-being.

Ray's mother had been reluctant to agree to additional support services for her son but appeared to understand the situation more clearly during the course of the conversations—that is, until Ms. Snow provided her information. Ms. Snow, a teacher who maintains classroom discipline with fear and intimidation and whose students seem to lag behind their peers in academic achievement, gave her report by saying, "I don't know what they are talking about. He is a perfect angel in my class. I think the other teachers just have it in for him. They are prejudiced against him and don't want him in their classes." According to the other assistant principal, Ray's mother, with her position confirmed and supported, ended the meeting with a refusal to consider alternative settings or services for her son. The other teachers left the meeting stunned that the system had apparently failed to address what they perceived to be the critical needs of a student, and they were equally dismayed at their colleague's remarks and apparent perceptions of their motivations.

Mr. Boston, one of the teachers at the meeting, sent an e-mail to Ms. Snow expressing his concern that she had made unfounded judgments about her colleagues and that her comments had undermined attempts to help a child with special needs. Ms. Snow fired back an angry response questioning his professionalism and his understanding and appreciation for diversity and reaffirming her conclusion that the real issue was the other teachers' attitudes toward Ray. A flurry of correspondence between the two ensued, with Ms. Snow sharing the messages with some of her colleagues by sending them carbon copies of the e-mails. By the end of the day, most of the faculty seemed to be aware of the building conflict, and many had taken sides, making judgments about a situation of which they knew little, other than what·was contained in the angry e-mails shared by Ms. Snow.

As your administrative colleague leaves your office, Mr. Boston arrives at your door. "We have to talk," he says.

Case Questions

1. Should you become involved in this situation? Why or why not?
2. What are the primary concerns that will likely be addressed in your conversation with Mr. Boston?
3. What advice will you give him regarding his future interactions with Ms. Snow?
4. What concerns might you address with Ms. Snow?
5. What steps, if any, might you take to resolve the conflict that has spread beyond Mr. Boston and Ms. Snow?

Suggested Activities

1. Does your school or school district have policies that address issues of professional communications or the use of e-mail? Design an insert for the teacher handbook that addresses such guidelines.
2. Talk with an experienced administrator in your district about the circumstances and ways in which an administrator might intervene to help resolve conflict between and among teachers in a school.
3. Develop your own set of guiding principles and a well-balanced plan of action that will help you encourage professional and civil communication and conflict resolution in your school community.

Problem 40: Out of Bounds in the Counselor's Office

You are an assistant principal in a small rural high school. As you return from lunch duty, you find on your desk a note from Ms. Muncie, the veteran guidance counselor. Notes from Ms. Muncie are rarely good news, and you spend a great deal of time smoothing the feathers of folks that she ruffles. She has an extraordinary knack, somewhat rare for an experienced guidance counselor, for saying exactly the wrong thing to exactly the wrong person.

The note concerns Lonnie Bloom, a withdrawn eleventh grader who has an increasingly erratic attendance record, who has been involved in several altercations with other girls on campus, and who routinely eats alone in the cafeteria. Ms. Muncie's note indicates that she has had a conversation with Lonnie at the request of her PE teacher, who is concerned about the girl's frequent unexcused tardiness. She reports that Lonnie regularly arrives too late to dress out and participate in class and is therefore in danger of failing. According to Ms. Muncie, when she asked Lonnie about this situation, Lonnie indicated that she feels uncomfortable in the locker room because the other students ridicule her because of her sexual orientation. She says that the teacher is aware of the harassment but does nothing to intervene.

Ms. Muncie goes on to say that she counseled Lonnie that she should expect that sort of treatment if she is going to flaunt her perversion in front of decent people and that she simply needs to keep those things to herself and get to class on time. According to the note, Lonnie argued that she had a right to feel safe in the locker room and that she had no intention of putting herself in that situation on a daily basis. Ms. Muncie indicates that she believes that she has done all that she can, has washed her hands of this matter, and is turning it over for you to handle as a discipline matter.

Case Questions

1. What issues will you address with the PE teacher and guidance counselor?
2. How will you deal with the student's attendance issue?
3. How will you determine whether this is an isolated incident or a widespread problem in your school?
4. What resources or trainings would you provide for faculty and staff to increase their awareness of and sensitivity to diversity?

Suggested Activities

1. Examine your school district's diversity and equal opportunity policies. Describe how you might go about training faculty and

staff about these policies and developing implementation plans or guidelines for your school.

2. Locate district and community resources that might provide appropriate support for students or employees protected by these policies, and make a plan for how you might disseminate this information to members of your school community.

Problem 41: The Inaccessible Principal

You are the superintendent of a small school district. There are only three schools in your district: one elementary school, one middle school, and one high school. You frequently visit the three schools and interact almost daily with students, teachers, noninstructional staff, administrators, and parents.

At the high school, Mr. Mitchell has been the principal for the last ten years. You have known Mr. Mitchell for twenty years. You were his principal when he taught elementary school. You have watched him develop over the years. He has been a vivacious and dynamic administrator. Lately, however, something is not quite right with Mr. Mitchell.

When you visit the high school, you notice that the two assistant principals are accessible and visible. Some of the teachers allude to a problem regarding Mr. Mitchell's availability. You have had at least three parents tell you that they had a difficult time when they tried to see Mr. Mitchell. When the school climate survey comes back, several people complain that Mr. Mitchell is always behind closed doors.

You know that Mr. Mitchell is dealing with major construction at his school. A new gymnasium is being built, as is a new wing of classrooms for special education students. You realize that dealing with architects and contractors can be time-consuming.

You decide to talk with Mr. Mitchell. When you ask him about the accessibility issue, he confides in you that he is just burned out. He explains that in addition to dealing with the construction, he has had to deal with two difficult marginal teachers. He further explains that he currently has a tough group of students in his eighth-grade class; these students are causing major disruptions that require significant time in dealing with them and their parents.

Case Questions

1. What could you as the superintendent have done to provide better support for this principal?
2. What should you say to the principal at this point?
3. How do you think the principal's lack of accessibility is affecting the school's culture?
4. What can you do at this point to help the principal?
5. What will you say to your constituents who complain about this principal?

Suggested Activities

1. Conduct research on stress as it relates to a career in school administration. Describe the major sources of stress that school principals face in performing their jobs.
2. Interview three current school administrators. Ask them to describe specific techniques that they use to manage stress. Write a summary of their responses.

COMMUNICATION SKILLS

Problem 42: "T-Shits"—A Principal Who Forgets a Critical Letter

It is three months into what promises to be a long and challenging school year. You are an assistant principal in a high school whose faculty and staff exhibit a low collective sense of efficacy. Even parents and students seem to feel that the school is the stepchild of the district. Your principal, Dr. Wong, an untested outsider to this tight-knit community, arrived last year following the sudden and unexpected departure of the much-beloved homegrown principal, who had held the position for more than a decade. After examining the school, Dr. Wong determined that he would seek recognition for the successes of the students and faculty by pursuing a national blue ribbon award from the Department of Education.

The veteran faculty members, many of whom resented the interloper, saw the application process as a product of the new principal's desire to seek personal glory. It did not help that his decision-making processes often appeared to favor the last person he had talked to and that faculty members formerly ostracized for overachieving appeared to be finding favor with the new administration, upsetting the age-old balance of powers. There were even rumors of impending lesson-plan checks and expectations that teachers actually show up for assigned duties. The fact that the school received the sought-after national award ahead of the crosstown rival high school did not impress the dedicated grumblers. They continue to scrutinize the principal's every move, hoping to find flaws with which they might dismiss his efforts to alter the culture of the school.

A former English teacher, Dr. Wong believes that good communication is the key to making the school effective. Each Monday, teachers receive a newsletter written by the principal himself, outlining upcoming deadlines and events, celebrating successes, and sharing teaching strategies. Teachers depend on the weekly updates and read them religiously. The first newsletter of the year, hot off the presses during the preschool teacher workshop days, contained a request that all faculty and staff wear the new spirit apparel that the principal has supplied for them to the district-opening convocation. The tops proudly displayed the school name and a copy of the symbol signifying the award. Dr. Wong, in a hurry that morning, used the spell-check feature on his computer but failed to read through the text. One error slipped though the cracks. In his convocation request he dropped the *r* from the word *t-shirt*.

Chuckles were audible in the office as teachers checked their mailboxes, and by lunchtime the entire faculty was aware of the embarrassing gaff. As the year progressed, this simple error seemed to take on a life of its own, becoming for the negative faculty members the rallying cry and excuse for dismissing the administrator's efforts to improve teaching practices and raise student achievement.

One afternoon before the start of a faculty meeting, you overhear several teachers engaged in a conversation about Dr. Wong's new "Reading, Writing, and Thinking across the Curriculum" initiative. The gist of the conversation is that they intend to present surface compliance but to resist the required pedagogical changes in hopes of undermining the program and thereby discrediting the principal. "That way," says one of the teachers to the amusement of her colleagues, "we won't have to wear any new t-shits." You are scheduled to meet with Dr. Wong and the other members of the administrative team in the morning to talk about staff morale and school climate. Given your observations, what will you share in the meeting?

Case Questions

1. What is the immediate problem?
2. What is the long-term problem (or problems)?
3. Is this issue simply a political power struggle? How does your assessment affect your strategy selection?
4. As an assistant principal and a member of the administrative team, what role must you play in addressing this situation?
5. What are possible negative consequences of addressing this situation directly?
6. Where would you advise the principal to begin?

Suggested Activities

1. Interview a principal who has worked with a school faculty to develop a positive culture to support student learning. Ask questions about the strategies he or she used, challenges encountered, and change effected.
2. With colleagues, discuss the relationships between teachers' resistance to change and school culture.

Problem 43: I Can't Believe She Wrote That!
An Assistant Principal Who Struggles with Communication

You are the principal at Bay Charter High School. This school has a diverse student population and a rich history of strong athletic teams. The parents have always been supportive of the school and the administrations' visions for academic excellence. You ask your new assistant principal, Ms. Dana Ross, to write the newsletter that will go home to parents the week before statewide testing starts. You ask Ms. Ross to specifically address tips for parents related to how they can prepare their children for the battery of Florida Comprehensive Assessment Tests. Ms. Ross gladly accepts the assignment and assures you that it will be taken care of. The phone rings in your office, and you rush to answer it with no further instructions for Ms. Ross to complete the assignment.

By the end of the week, numerous parents start calling the school wanting to meet with you to discuss the latest newsletter they received from Bay Charter High School. You ask your secretary to provide you with a copy of the newsletter that went home with all 680 students at the school. As you read the letter that Ms. Ross composed, printed, and sent home with every student, you realize that you have a huge problem to deal with. The following are a few excerpts from the newsletter that caused concerns with the parents:

- Parents should not allow their children to attend any athletic practices during the week of statewide testing because they need to be completely rested and mentally sharp for the academic rigors of the high-stakes testing program.
- Parents should not feed their children foods that cause gas (such as beans and broccoli) because this creates a distraction and disruption during critical test-taking periods.
- Parents should hydrate their children before sending them to school because the tests are timed and students will not receive hall passes to go to the water fountain during testing.
- Parents should be sure that their children wear neutral-colored clothing during the week of testing so as not to draw attention away from the testing focus.
- Parents should consider keeping their children home from late-evening church services during the week of testing so that the children can get to bed before 9:00 PM.

Case Questions

1. As the principal, can you defend these specific tips for parents that are in this newsletter?

2. What are some of the problems or concerns that you can expect to hear from the large number of parents who have requested to see you?
3. How will you deal with these parents as they come to see you about their concerns?
4. Is this all Ms. Ross's fault? Please explain.
5. How will you deal with Ms. Ross to prevent such incidents from happening again?
6. Does Ms. Ross's handling of the newsletter incident warrant punishment? If so, please explain?
7. Should you inform the superintendent about this incident? Why or why not?
8. What schoolwide strategies will you put into place to prevent this type of problem from occurring again?
9. What affect might Ms. Ross's newsletter have on the positive relations between the school and the community?

Suggested Activities

Using the Interstate School Leaders Licensure Consortium or the Educational Leadership Constituent Council Standards as your frame, select two of the following activities and develop them fully, based on the case information provided:

1. What steps might you take to promote or enhance Ms. Ross's multicultural awareness related to racial and ethnic sensitivity?
2. Devise a written communication strategy for all outgoing correspondences from the school that will ensure that the message is appropriate for the intended audience and that the message exhibits sensitivity and respect for a diverse population.
3. Formulate a team of educational personnel within the school that can help monitor all outgoing written correspondences that will allow for consistency and trustworthiness of the messages being sent.
4. Determine a verbal statement that you as the principal might share with the faculty and staff to explain the unfortunate incident and still allow Ms. Ross to save face with her colleagues.

REFLECTIVE QUESTIONS

1. Why is it imperative that school leaders have exemplary interpersonal skills?

2. How effective are you as a communicator—in speech and in writing?

3. When do you believe that it is appropriate for a school leader to act as a mediator between faculty? Please explain.

4. Describe the sources of stress that you think will affect you as a school leader.

5. How will you deal with stress as a school leader?

6. To what extent do you feel that the career development of subordinates is the responsibility of a school leader? Please explain.

CHAPTER 8

Financial Management and Resource Allocation

Educational Leadership Constituent Council Standard 8—Financial Management and Resource Allocation specifies that the institution's program prepares school leaders who demonstrate an understanding of and the capacity to identify and analyze the major sources of fiscal and nonfiscal resources for schools and school districts; acquire and manage financial and material assets and capital goods and services, allocating resources according to district or school priorities; develop an efficient budget-planning process that is driven by district and school priorities and that involves staff and the community; and perform budget management functions, including financial planning, monitoring, cost control, expenditures accounting, and cash flow management.

An effective school administrator must be a good steward of the resources of the school, the district, and the community. Understanding and identifying the fiscal and human resources available to the school and marshalling them effectively to support student learning strengthens the culture of learning within a school and does so in a systematic and purposeful way. But developing an efficient budget-planning process that is driven by student learning needs as well as school and district priorities and is responsive to community values and expectations is critical. Involving school community members in the processes and educating them about those processes, the possibilities, and the challenges also needs to occur.

High-performing leaders develop the technical knowledge needed to effectively monitor and organize the acquisition and management of financial and material assets, as well as capital goods and services to support school priorities. They must also possess strong visioning, decision-making, and communication skills. From the bookkeeper who manages the cash flow to the teacher who collects field-trip fees, all faculty and staff members must be on the same page; but developing a common vision of the goals and priorities is a process that is not without political maneuvering and potential conflict. It is here that the school administrator may encounter some of the greatest challenges.

The savvy administrator will identify and develop key personnel within the faculty and staff to ensure that resources are managed appropriately and allocated to achieve the school's specific curricular and instructional goals. Attention to the details of the daily operations of the school and the establishment of clear procedures and expectations must go hand in hand with the cooperative budget development processes if long- and short-range strategic goals and priorities are to be met.

In this chapter you will encounter common challenges faced by school leaders on a daily basis. From the financial secretary with marginal skills but powerful political connections to the factions who struggle for control over resources and the ethical issues surrounding individuals' special interests, you will grapple with issues that not only call for a knowledge of policy and the technical skills involved in managing and allocating financial resources but require you to consider your role as a community builder and an active shaper of school climate and culture. As you read and consider these cases, focus on the connections between the management of resources and the overall charge of developing, articulating, and implementing a shared vision that can be supported by the larger organization and the school community. How do your decision-making and partnership building skills come into play as you tackle the challenges of financial management? Consider your own strengths and the skills that will enable you to be proactive in the planning and management processes, and identify ways in which you can strengthen your ability to be an effective and ethical steward of your school's resources.

Problem 44: Pizza Party Every Friday—
Handling a Parent-Teacher Association Proposal

The Parent-Teacher Association (PTA) for New Horizon Elementary School approached you, the principal, about a fund-raising campaign to replace the outdated computers in the computer labs. The PTA is a powerful organization within the New Horizon community and has always provided for the school. Technology is highly valued by the parents and teachers.

The teachers have complained to the teacher's union about the lack of adequate computers for instruction. The union representatives have met with the school district and the PTA members in an effort to get financial support from the district. The school district has not recognized technology issues as a budget priority. The district has allocated large sums of money to build a new school. The union supports the efforts of the PTA, and there is a strong united front to make this project go at your school.

The PTA plans to have a pizza party at New Horizon every Friday after the State Comprehensive Assessment Tests have been completed. The PTA plans to sell pizza and soda to the children during the last thirty minutes of the school day. A local pizza company will donate half of the pizzas and sodas to the PTA as long as the PTA agrees to hand out discount coupons to all students. The PTA will sell one slice of pizza and a cup of soda for one dollar each.

The estimated profit for this fund-raising project will yield approximately ten thousand dollars. This money will be deposited directly into the PTA account. The PTA Board of Directors will purchase computers from a reputable computer company at a fraction of the retail cost. This fund-raising project will enable the PTA to replace twenty outdated computers in the lab.

Case Questions

1. How will you handle this fund-raising proposal from the powerful PTA organization?
2. Describe the advantages and disadvantages of this fund-raising activity.
3. Does the fact that the teacher's union supports this fund-raising activity concern you? Why or why not?
4. Do you believe the superintendent will support the fund-raising project? Explain you answer.
5. How could this fund-raising activity affect other issues within your school, such as instruction, custodial staff, and student safety?

Suggested Activities

Using the Interstate School Leaders Licensure Consortium or the Educational Leadership Constituent Council Standards as your frame, select two of the following activities and develop them fully, based on the case information provided:

1. Write a three-page paper describing the moral and ethical implications that you must consider before making your decision related to the fund-raising project?
2. Write a three-page paper where you identify and analyze the major sources of fiscal and nonfiscal resources that might be used to replace outdated computers.
3. Write a three-page paper where you describe an efficient budget-planning process that is driven by the district and school priorities and that involves the staff and community.
4. Create a written plan that describes how you would formulate a committee of educational and community personnel to address the school district's need to manage financial and material assets and allocate resources based on individual school needs.

Problem 45: Deal or No Deal? Controversy Surrounding the Exclusive Use of a Private Vendor

The Athletic Booster Club president, Bo Matte, grew up in the Evangeline community, lettered in three sports, and graduated in the top 10 percent of his senior class. Bo owns a large insurance company in the large city just six miles away from the Evangeline School District, where his three children have attended. His wife, Jen, is a first-grade teacher in the elementary school and has never taught at another school in her eighteen-year career as an educator. Bo and the superintendent of the Evangeline School District attend the same church, and both are members of the exclusive golf country club that just opened in their community.

The Athletic Booster Club is a powerful organization within the community. Sports are viewed as a major part of the school. Organized competitive sports programs start when children enter the first grade. The number of season-ticket holders far out number the yearly totals of parent conferences at the three community schools combined.

For the past several months, Bo has been working with the local Pepski Company, a large soft drink distributor in the area. Ron is the chief executive officer of Pepski Company. Bo and Ron want to come up with an exclusive ten-year deal that will benefit both organizations. Ron is a sharp businessman with many contacts, and he knows how to play the game. Bo and Ron have reached a tentative agreement. The Evangeline High School Athletic Booster Club will give Pepski Company exclusive rights to sell its products at all athletic events for the next ten years in exchange for a one-time contribution to the athletic program of $1.89 million. In addition, new lights for the athletic fields located on the school property will be installed by the Pepski Company. Lastly, vending machines will be placed throughout the three schools, and the athletic department will be able to keep 40 percent of the profits.

The Athletic Booster Club members unanimously approved the deal at their last meeting. Bo, knowing that such a deal would require school board approval, invited the superintendent to the meeting to hear the details of this ten-year agreement. All principals and teachers were invited to this meeting as well. Another interesting fact is that the superintendent's wife recently won and took possession of a new Ranger bass boat from the Athletic Booster Club as part of its annual raffle to raise money.

Several teachers and community people have argued against such a deal. The grounds for their arguments have been based on student health. These opponents have described medical research that highlights the detrimental impact of junk food and drinks that are high in sugar and caffeine. The elementary principal, a former coach, has argued that the schools should receive the 40 percent profit to help strengthen the decline in instructional budgets that all schools were experiencing. The elementary principal has added that it is difficult to support this deal entirely when many of the classrooms have outdated computers and textbooks that are in poor condition. The middle school principal has expressed concern that the vending machine will interfere with the cafeteria's function and that there might be some legal issues to consider as well. During the meeting, however, most of the people present were in favor of the deal and exploded with a cacophony of objections for those who argued against it.

Case Questions

1. How could a needs assessment help strengthen or identify potential solutions?
2. List some of the reasons that the teachers and community people might have for arguing against the deal that the elementary principal suggested.
3. Do you believe the superintendent will support the agreement? Explain you answer.
4. Assuming that the superintendent will support this deal, list several things that he should consider before he makes a recommendation to the school board asking its favorable approval.
5. Predict how the school board members might vote on this issue.
6. List the pros and cons on how this decision could affect the curriculum at this community school.

Suggested Activities

Using the Interstate School Leaders Licensure Consortium or the Educational Leadership Constituent Council Standards as your frame, select two of the following activities and develop it fully, based on the case information provided:

1. Identify and analyze the positive and negative benefits that the deal would bring to the schools and the school district.
2. Review your school district's food service policy. Devise a written communication strategy for addressing the food service concerns that the deal may violate.
3. Formulate a team of educational and community personnel that might address the school district's declining fiscal resources dedicated to instructional programs.
4. Determine the value of an oversight committee to ensure the money acquired from the deal is used properly.

Problem 46: Just Trying to Make a Living—
A Coach with a Conflict of Interest

You are the new principal of a high school. Your superintendent heavily encouraged the retirement of your predecessor because she was burned out and had put the school on autopilot.

You have been leading the school since January. During this time, you have started to get to know your faculty. One faculty member, Coach Rob, is the boys' varsity baseball coach. He is an excellent coach who has clear expectations, a great sense of humor, and is a wonderful motivator. The students and parents love him. The team has had another great season, with fifteen wins and only two losses.

As summer approaches, Coach Rob hangs flyers around the school and sends out blanket e-mails to faculty, students, and community members advertising his private baseball camp. In his communications, Coach Rob excitedly recruits teenagers for his four-week summer baseball camp. He explains that the camp will take place on school grounds, and he lists a fee of $425 per student.

During this same period, you get a phone call from the director of the local recreation department. She asks you if she can lease some of your athletic fields during the summer for recreation summer camps. She asks to specifically use the baseball field. You tell her that you will get back to her within a week.

You call in Coach Rob to ask him some questions about his summer baseball camp. You find out that he has had similar camps for the last five years. In the past, he has used the school's athletic facilities and equipment and has not paid a dime to lease the facilities. All of the monies gained from the summer camp fees went directly into Coach Rob's pocket. When you ask him if he has ever considered that this practice was a conflict of interest for the school, he states, "I'm just trying to make a living."

Case Questions

1. Is it appropriate for Coach Rob to advertise his private summer baseball camp using school bulletin boards and school e-mail? Why or why not?

2. What are the advantages and disadvantages of letting Coach Rob use the school's facilities without paying to lease?
3. Who would you allow to use the facilities during the summer?
4. How do you justify your answer to question 3?
5. How does the fact that Coach Rob is an excellent coach affect your decision? Please explain.

Suggested Activity

Research your school district's policies on leasing school facilities and conflicts of interest. Write a three-page paper explaining how you would apply these policies to the given situation.

**Problem 47: A Grant Gone Bad—
Teachers Who Don't Follow Through**

Note: The following case study was submitted by graduate students Maureen Mitchell and Kim Richards and edited by Lynette Fields.

You are a principal at a middle school. Your school consists of approximately twelve hundred students, fifty-five teachers, and forty support staff members. Your school was chosen by the district office to participate in a $400,000 technology grant. If your school should accept and participate, it will receive twenty hours of on-site training for teachers by a technology specialist from the Center for Instructional Technology, sixty iBook laptop computers, three mobile carts to store the laptops, one overhead digital projector, a computer-based math lab with thirty-five student computer stations and thirty-five computer desks, and a multitude of software.

The written information about the grant is distributed to the faculty and staff by Ms. Mason, your school's technology specialist. You advise your faculty and staff that they will vote at the next faculty meeting, in two weeks, on whether they would like to participate in the grant. The faculty and staff know that if they do not complete twenty hours of training, the school will lose all of the equipment that it will receive. The vote takes place, and it is unanimous. Everyone wants to participate in the grant.

During the summer hiring process, you make sure that every candidate is aware of the training that he or she has to commit to upon accepting the job. Each new teacher agrees to participate and commit to the twenty hours of training.

Your computers and labs arrive in July. The math teacher is excited about her new lab and is ready for the students to arrive in August. The technology specialist sets up a schedule for teachers to check out the mobile lab. Ms. Mason, the technology specialist, also creates a schedule for the teachers to begin their training during preplanning. Things seem to be going smoothly until October. Ms. Mason lets you know that forty-two of the fifty-five teachers have not been to any training. She has tried to encourage them to come because if they miss too many, they will not have enough time to get the twenty hours in before the end of the year. At the next faculty meeting, you remind the faculty of their commitment to technology training regarding the grant. Ms. Mason also reminds them that the district will take back the equipment and discontinue the training if the school does not meet the requirements of the grant. You go to the technology training in November and see that only three teachers are present.

Case Questions

1. How will you handle this situation?
2. What will you say to the teachers who are not going to training?
3. At what point will you contact the district?
4. What will you say to the district when you do make contact?
5. What type of disciplinary action, if any, will you give to the teachers?

Suggested Activity

Write a short paper explaining the processes and procedures that you would have put into place to monitor financial, material, and human resources related to this grant.

Problem 48: Counting on Bettysue—
A School Bookkeeper Who Drops the Ball

You are a high school principal in a rural district. You have been in your position for one year, but your bookkeeper, Bettysue, the superintendent's sister-in-law, has held her position for more than fifteen years under four different administrations. She is knowledgeable about the political land-scape of the district and even more knowledgeable about the personal lives of the various members of the school community but has little for-mal training in accounting.

Your predecessor found that Bettysue's propensity to gossip was so persistent that it interfered with her ability to conduct school business during office hours. Her desk was always an unsightly mess, and on nu-merous occasions, she made errors, depositing funds into incorrect ac-counts and holding cash in an unsecured desk drawer for up to a week, at a time when she forgot to make regular deposits. Transferring her to a different position or to a different school was not an option, and so he had a partition erected around Bettysue's workstation to reduce dis-tractions so that she could better perform her job. The result, however, made Bettysue mobile. You have found that she is rarely at her desk and can often be found in one of the teacher workrooms catching up on the latest news or sharing confidential information about students and teachers with parent volunteers.

You have made your expectations clear to Bettysue regarding her job tasks. You have had several conversations with her about professional-ism and maintaining confidentiality about student discipline and per-sonnel matters, but she has blatantly ignored your suggestions and di-rectives. This morning, one of your secretaries informed you that Bettysue had paid an office supply vendor in cash from the Athletic Booster Club's receipts from the previous night's basketball game con-cessions. When your secretary questioned the exchange, Bettysue indi-cated that she would "juggle things to make it all come out even at the end of the day." As you summon the energy to have another conversa-tion with your bookkeeper, you open an envelope containing the dis-trict auditor's report for your school. In the report, auditors have cited twenty-seven violations of policy and noted several irregular practices. The attached note indicates that you need to be prepared to discuss the report with the superintendent at the principal's meeting on Friday.

Case Questions

1. How will you approach your conversation with the superintend-ent?

2. What will you say in your discussion with Bettysue?

3. What do your district's policies and procedures outline as appropriate courses of action in this situation?

4. What resources would you have available in your district that would help you address the issues outlined in this case?

5. Does Bettysue's relationship with the superintendent affect the way in which you will work with her to bring her job performance into compliance with district policy and acceptable professionalism? If so, how?

Suggested Activities

1. Review the state law and district policy that address the handling of financial affairs in your current school; then interview a principal, an individual from your district's budget office, and a financial secretary or bookkeeper from a local school about processes and procedures for monitoring and maintaining good business management practices at the school level. Create a checklist and quick reference guide that would help you train and monitor a new bookkeeper or financial secretary for a school similar to your current assignment.

2. Prepare a presentation for an audience consisting of teachers and support staff members to explain the financial management processes and procedures in place in your school. Be sure to include information about the policies, the rationale for the procedures, the resources available to assist them in complying with the policies and procedures, and a "quick guide" handout to consult throughout the school year.

Problem 49: He Just Can't Say "No"— An Assistant Principal Who Overspends the Textbook Budget

You are the principal of a middle school. You have two assistant principals. The personalities and styles of the two assistant principals are quite different. Mr. Morris is organized, detailed oriented, and has excellent interpersonal skills. Mr. Bradley has a heart of gold, is extremely reliable and loyal, but is a more random type of thinker. At the end of each academic year, in an effort to professionally develop your assistant principals, you redistribute job tasks. One of the major changes for the upcoming academic year is that Mr. Bradley is going to take over textbooks. He will be responsible for the textbook budget, which includes making purchases. Mr. Morris was somewhat tight with the monies and has accumulated $140,000.

When the faculty and staff hear that Mr. Bradley is the new manager of textbooks, they hit him with multiple requests. You remind Mr. Bradley to follow the district textbook adoption cycle. For the upcoming academic year, it is time to update the materials in the area of language arts. You make an unfortunate false assumption that Mr. Bradley understands budgeting.

During the summer, you begin to notice boxes piling up in the front office. When you take a closer look, you realize that these are textbook deliveries.

When you ask Mr. Bradley how things are going in regard to textbooks, you notice that his face turns red. He explains that he just realized that he has overspent the textbook budget.

You are concerned because those monies were to be spent cautiously and carefully over the next three years. When you analyze what Mr. Bradley spent, you find the following:

Sixth-grade language arts texts	$38,000
Seventh-grade language arts texts	$40,000
Eighth-grade language arts texts	$42,000
Spelling books, all grade levels	$20,000
Accelerated reading books	$2,000
Handwriting books	$2,000

Case Questions

1. What do you say to Mr. Bradley?
2. How could you have been a better mentor to Mr. Bradley?
3. Who are you going to notify at the district office? For what purpose?
4. What can you do to correct this problem at this point?

Suggested Activity

Write a short paper that explains typical steps that one should address as he or she develops a financial plan for purchasing textbooks.

REFLECTIVE QUESTIONS

1. What are the major activities that need to occur when developing a budget?
2. How can you involve staff and the community in budget planning?
3. What are the school leader's responsibilities in terms of fiscal accounting?
4. What computer programs are you aware of that would be especially helpful in managing the school's budget and its supplies and equipment?
5. What resources are available to you in your search for financial and material assets?
6. Describe the processes that you will use to monitor your bookkeeper.

CHAPTER 9

Technology and Information Services

Educational Leadership Constituent Council Standard 9—Technology and Information Systems specifies that the institution's program prepares school leaders who demonstrate an understanding of and the capability to use technology, telecommunications, and information systems to enrich curriculum and instruction; apply and assess current technologies for school management and business procedures; develop and monitor long-range plans for school and district technology and information systems, making informed decisions about computer hardware and software and about staff development, keeping in mind the impact of technologies on student outcomes and school operations.

Keeping pace with the rapid changes in technology is a difficult challenge for school administrators today. In addition, school leaders must adjust to and prepare for transformations that occur in society and education.

It is important for school leaders to meet these challenges. Schools thrive on information and are a reflection of what is occurring in society. When administrators align technology with their school mission and goals, good things happen. Technology helps school leaders improve student achievement, accountability, resource acquisition, and professional development.

What are some critical tasks that administrators should perform in the area of technology? First, school leaders should develop a technology plan with short-term and long-term goals. This plan should be developed with the assistance of faculty, staff, and school community members. The plan should include ways to identify and access additional funding sources for technological needs. Second, once funds are acquired, appropriate technological resources should be provided to teachers, staff, and students. Third, school leaders should support professional development opportunities for their faculty and staff to encourage individual growth and daily usage of technology for instruction. Fourth, school leaders should create, implement, and monitor appropriate policies and procedures for technology usage. Fifth and final, school leaders should be excellent role models for technology usage, using technology to encourage communication and collaboration.

In the cases that follow, you will get the opportunity to practice many of the critical tasks outlined. You will get the chance to problem-solve situations where teachers and staff hoard resources, are afraid of change, and use technology inappropriately. You will also be presented with a situation where, as a new principal, you have a sufficient technology budget but must develop both a long-term and a short-term plan for your new school.

USING TECHNOLOGY TO ENRICH THE CURRICULUM

Problem 50: Computers in the Closet—
A Teacher Who Has Resources but Chooses Not to Use Them

Note: The following case study was submitted by graduate student Peggy Ross and edited by Lynette Fields.

You are a new principal of a school. One of your many tasks is the evaluation of teachers. Tammy Wilson, one of your teachers, has a reputation for being an outstanding teacher and has been your school's curriculum technology integration teacher for the past two years.

In her role as curriculum technology integration teacher, Ms. Wilson received the following equipment: two desktop computers, two laptop computers, a printer, a scanner, and a digital camera. In addition, she received sixty hours of training. Upon completion of her training, Ms. Wilson is supposed to teach other teachers at your school what she has learned regarding the integration of technology into the curriculum.

When you have observed or walked through Ms. Wilson's room, you have noticed the two desktop computers. The computers were off, and there was not any evidence of technology usage. When you ask Ms. Wilson where the other equipment is, she opens the closet door and says, "I just haven't had time to set up everything. Don't worry. The equipment is secure in this locked closet."

You have had three teachers who actively use technology asking for additional resources, such as laptops and a scanner. These and other teachers have also requested additional professional development in the area of technology integration. When you ask if Ms. Wilson has provided any training, they reply, "No." In addition, there is currently a freeze on your technology budget, so no new equipment can be purchased from this budget.

Today, a parent called you. She wanted to know why the computers in Ms. Wilson's room are never turned on. She states that her daughter is anxious to use the brand new computers.

Case Questions

1. There are several problems here. How will you prioritize these issues?
2. When you conference with Ms. Wilson, what will you say to her?
3. How do you respond to the parent's concern?
4. How will you address the technological needs of the teachers at your school?

Suggested Activities

1. Create a plan of support to help Ms. Wilson use technology in her classroom.
2. Assist Ms. Wilson in creating a plan to provide professional development to the other teachers in your school.
3. Help Ms. Wilson design a system for sharing her technological resources with other teachers.
4. Develop a plan to find additional funding sources to provide technological equipment and professional development for your school. Be specific about who is to be involved and what tasks they would be expected to accomplish.

Problem 51: Hesitant Henrietta—A Teacher Afraid of Change

Note: The following case study was submitted by graduate student Evelyn Mowatt and edited by Lynette Fields.

You are the principal of an elementary school. You have one assistant principal. You do not have an instructional technology specialist at your school. One of your major tasks is the evaluation of teachers.

Henrietta Holcomb has been a fourth-grade classroom teacher for twenty years. She has always been respected by her peers, students, and their parents; she has been complimented for being creative and exciting. Many parents request Henrietta as a teacher for their children.

Henrietta is fearful of technology. Although she has a desktop computer in her classroom, she is one of the few teachers who still does not use e-mail to communicate with others within the school. She has attended professional development trainings on technology but is the first to admit that she just is not comfortable teaching with computers.

You have monitored the standardized test scores of all your teachers. You have noticed a trend in the last five years. Henrietta's students do not perform well on the technology portion of the standardized test.

Case Questions

1. When you conference with Henrietta, what are you going to say?
2. How can you support Henrietta in the usage of technology in her classroom?
3. Since Henrietta is a beloved teacher of the school and community, how will you prevent or deal with negative feelings from others as you assist Henrietta?
4. How will you document Henrietta's progress?

Suggested Activity

Review your district's goals and policies on teacher usage of technology in the classroom. In addition, review national standards for teacher integration of technology. Create a plan that explains how you will move all of your instructional staff members toward weekly or daily use of technology in their instruction.

MONITORING COMPUTER USAGE

Problem 52: Lloyd Who Lacks Follow-Through—
An Assistant Principal Who Does Not Do His Homework

Note: The following case study was submitted by graduate student Peggy Ross and edited by Lynette Fields.

You are the principal of an elementary school. You have one assistant principal, Lloyd Berbecker. Lloyd has been an assistant principal at your school for fifteen years. Lloyd loves children and is an easygoing person with a kind heart and a great sense of humor. On the other hand, Lloyd lacks organizational skills.

Lloyd approaches you with a problem. He explains that Teddy, a boy who is physically and cognitively impaired in one of the first-grade varying exceptionalities classes, needs a computer. Lloyd further explains that the Individual Education Plan Team, of which Lloyd is a member, wrote an individual education plan that suggests that Teddy needs a computer in class and at home for schoolwork.

You respond that Mr. Van Dyke, the instructional technology specialist, just received four brand new laptops from a grant. You suggest that Lloyd see Mr. Van Dyke. You tell Lloyd that you want a written contract signed by Teddy's parent or guardian regarding any computer loan, and you want Lloyd to develop guidelines for monitoring home use of the computer. Lloyd states that those are wonderful ideas.

About two weeks go by, and a problem is brought to your attention. The teaching aid from the first-grade varying exceptionalities class is waiting to see you. She has a laptop in her hands. She shows you that Teddy's father has been using the computer for his lawn maintenance business and that someone has been visiting pornographic websites on this computer.

When you ask Lloyd about the contract and guidelines, Lloyd produces the contract but states that he forgot to develop the guidelines. When you ask if Lloyd or anyone else has been monitoring the home usage of the laptop, Lloyd says, "No."

Case Questions

1. What do you say to Lloyd at this point?
2. How are you going to gather facts about this situation? From whom?
3. How are you going to deal with the inappropriate use of the laptop?
4. Are you going to delegate this problem to Lloyd? Why or why not?
5. While you are solving the problem, are you going to allow Teddy to take home a computer? Why or why not?

Suggested Activity

Create a plan to facilitate home usage of school technology by students. Describe specific expectations. Describe specific strategies for monitoring. Describe how inappropriate use of technology will be dealt with.

Problem 53: Who Is That Mystery Person?
A Custodian Who Surfs the Net Inappropriately

Note: The following case study was submitted by graduate student Richard Bessey and edited by Lynette Fields.

You are an assistant principal of a school. Some of your major tasks include maintaining the plant and facility, supervising the custodial staff, and monitoring technology and information systems of your school.

Mr. O'Hara has been a teacher at your school for fifteen years. He is known as an excellent social studies teacher. His performance appraisals have been outstanding. He is also known, however, as being a loner with few friends. He spends most of his day in his classroom.

Your technology specialist, Ms. Nanns, comes to see you. One of her tasks is to monitor the visited websites on school computers. She states that someone has used the computer in Mr. O'Hara's classroom to visit pornographic websites. She further explains that this activity seems to be happening in the evening.

When you call in Mr. O'Hara to investigate this matter, he is shocked. He vehemently denies any part of this problem. He states emphatically that he would never do anything like that to compromise his contract, certificate, or profession. You ask Mr. O'Hara and Ms. Nanns to not discuss this problem with anyone.

You decide to set up security cameras to monitor Mr. O'Hara's computer within his classroom. One of the videotapes reveals a newly hired custodian entering the room and using the computer to visit pornographic websites. When the computer history is retrieved, it shows that pornographic sites were logged at the same time as the custodian was in the room on the videotape.

Case Questions

1. Will you continue to investigate this matter, or is this sufficient information upon which to take action?
2. Will you confer with your principal or anyone specific at the district office before you meet with the custodian? Why?
3. What district or school policies/rules were violated?
4. Will you confer with your head plant manager, the custodian's immediate supervisor? Why or why not?
5. What will you say to Mr. O'Hara?
6. Will you make this incident public knowledge? Why or why not?

Suggested Activity

Investigate district and school guidelines. Write a paper describing the bases for termination of noninstructional employees within your school district.

LONG-RANGE PLANS FOR SCHOOL TECHNOLOGY

Problem 54: Where Do I Begin? A Principal of a New School Making Decisions about Technology

You were recently hired to be the principal of Aspen Carlton Charter School, an elementary school. The contractors are just finishing construction of a beautiful facility. Every classroom was wired for Internet access, SMART boards, and projection systems. There is a state-of-the-art media center with room for a small computer lab that is prewired.

To be eligible to attend this school, students must live within the prestigious community Aspen Carlton Estates. Students whose parents work at Aspen Carlton Estates are also eligible to attend this school. The board of this school has made it very clear to you that they want to emphasize technology in the curriculum of this school.

When the school opens in seven months, it will have two classes at each grade level, kindergarten through fifth grade. You are responsible for hiring teachers and a media specialist who are technologically savvy, and you are responsible for purchasing all of the technological hardware and software for the school.

Case Questions

1. Many things need to be done. What are your first three priorities? Why?
2. Name three people or positions that you could use as a resource to help you make decisions.
3. How will you decide which companies to use for the purchase of hardware and software?
4. Create five interview questions that you would use to ascertain the technological expertise of a potential hire?
5. What additional resources do you need to be ready in seven months?

Suggested Activities

1. Create a technology plan for your first year. Assume that you have a budget of $1 million to acquire the following: professional development, Internet access, hardware (computers, printers, SMART boards, and projection systems), audiovisual supplies, and software. What would you purchase or implement in fifteen classrooms and a media center?

2. Create a long-range plan for the next two to five years. What would be your goals? How would you implement those goals?

REFLECTIVE QUESTIONS

1. How proficient are you in the area of technology?
2. To what extent are you comfortable being a role model of technology? Please explain.
3. What factors will you consider in creating a long-term technology plan for your school or district?
4. What do you believe to be the advantages and disadvantages to using technology as an instructional tool?
5. What strategies will you use to monitor technology within your school or building?

CHAPTER 10

Community and Media Relations

Educational Leadership Constituent Council Standard 10—Community and Media Relations specifies that the institution's program prepares school leaders who demonstrate an understanding of and the capability to analyze community and district power structures and identify major opinion leaders and their relationships to school goals and programs; articulate the district's or school's vision, mission, and priorities to the community and media and build community support for district or school priorities and programs; communicate effectively with various cultural, ethnic, racial, and special interest groups in the community; involve family and community in appropriate policy development, program planning, and assessment processes; develop an effective and interactive staff-communications plan and public relations program; and utilize and respond effectively to electronic and printed news media.

Establishing and maintaining effective school-community relations is one of the most important tasks that an educational leader performs. In essence, planning for and developing these relationships is a function of social accountability. As educators, we are answerable or accountable to all of the publics we serve—those within the school setting and those in the broader community. School and community relations planning are not simply about deciding what one wants to communicate or how one wants the school to be perceived. It is also not a collection of strategies, techniques, approaches, or tricks of the trade. Instead, it has a broader purpose; it is about how we communicate about our accountability to the students, teachers, parents and caregivers, and the community members, who all have a stake in providing quality educational opportunities to all children.

This role has never been more important. In the twenty-first century, we find that in any given community there are far more households without children in our schools than with. How these non-school-affiliated community members and business leaders frame their opinions about public schools is often more of a function of what they hear in the media than what they know from firsthand experiences and communications. The message that confronts them is one of dropout rates, incidences of violence, poor test scores, and political calls for reform that decry the state of public education nationwide. For those who have daily contact with dedicated teachers and motivated students, most would have a hard time recognizing their schools in the picture that the media and politicians paint. Helping the community develop a realistic sense of the challenges, successes, and opportunities present in our schools is the role of an effective community relations plan. Good communication generates support for the schools' visions, missions, and goals.

It is not realistic for a school administrator to become a one-person public relations firm, nor is it appropriate. Administrators cannot and should not go it alone. Developing two-way communications between and among internal publics (faculty, staff, students) and external publics that the school serves (parents and caregivers, community members, businesspeople, and policymakers) requires a systematic involvement of key communicators that come from each of the aforementioned groups. Understanding the power structures within the community and the school system and developing a proactive responsive course of action is critical. When a leader makes effective communications a priority, she or he sets the stage for a useful exchange of information, feedback, and assistance that support collaborative continual improvement, which in turn benefits students.

The effective school leader understands the goals and objectives of school and community relationship building and therefore plans to systematically develop multidirectional channels of communication. He or she must not only identify all of the publics with whom the school must communicate but must also determine how the communication will be carried out. As a leader, she or he must consider when, how, how much, and how often conversations should take place and must then engage the appropriate stakeholders in the processes. Continual monitoring and adjusting are a given, as community expectations and understandings are fluid and misinformation abounds. The school leader sets the tone, the expectations, and the parameters for the strategic communications of a school.

In this chapter you will be asked to consider scenarios in which administrators' skills are tested as they wrestle with rumor control, public power plays by politically connected employees, and the challenges of working with the media. As you read and react to each of these situations, consider ways in which you as an administrator will plan for developing clear lines of communication and healthy school and community relations.

Problem 55: From Heaven to Hell—A New Band Director Who Clashes with Parents and the Community

You are the principal at a middle school or high school. Recently the band director, Rick Anderson, who had been the band director at your school for seven years, moves to another county. Rick was a top-notch band director who was greatly respected by students and parents. The community thought highly of him as well. He had created a music mentor program where he paired the top student performers with a musical mentor in the community.

One of your assistant principals hires Allen Martin to replace Rick. Allen is an experienced band director from another part of the county who was highly recommended by his principal. Allen, however, wants to create his own unique program, and he makes no apologies for several swift changes. He eliminates the music mentor program. He also uses sarcastic humor in an attempt to motivate students. As a result, you and the other assistant principal receive several phone calls from upset parents and community members. When you sit in on parent conferences, you notice that Allen smirks and is quite abrupt with parents. Again, he makes no apologies for the things that he wants to change. Several students, parents, and community members call the local newspaper about their complaints. A scathing article is written that expresses the overall dissatisfaction with Allen's leadership as the band director.

Case Questions

1. How will you de-escalate the situation?
2. How will you deal with the way that Allen acts in parent conferences?
3. How will you more actively supervise the transition from Rick's leadership to Allen's?
4. If Allen objects to your advice or directives in regard to the transition, what are your next steps?

Suggested Activities

1. Create a list of interview questions for hiring a band director.
2. Write a response that you would publish in the local newspaper to the scathing article.

Problem 56: Extra! Extra! Read All about It— The Coach Who Creates Negative Publicity by Using a Racial Slur

You are the principal of a large middle school in a small town. A popular hometown boy is now the physical education teacher who coaches the school's football team. The coach takes a personal interest in an economically disadvantaged African American player. Knowing that the student cannot afford the cleats he needs to play with, the teacher arranges for a local sporting goods store to donate the needed equipment. The coach goes to the student's homeroom to find out the appropriate shoe size. He asks the teacher for permission to speak to the student, identifying him by his first name. As there are two students in the class with the same first name, the teacher asks the coach to specify which student he needs to see. The coach, according to the teacher, identifies the student as "the dark one."

The homeroom teacher shares the incident with other teachers and with an African American guidance counselor who is politically active in the community, where racial tensions have historically run high. Before the matter is brought to the attention of the school administration, the counselor takes the information into the community, and over the weekend the local newspaper prints the story. At eight o'clock on Monday morning, you return from an out-of-town trip to find an office lobby full of angry parents, teachers, and community members, the student's grandparents and their attorney, and a message to call the superintendent as soon as possible. You look out of the window of your office in time to see a broadcast van from the local television station pull into the bus loop in front of the school.

Case Questions

1. What are the significant issues you will need to address, and in what order will you address them?
2. What will you say to each of the parties who wish to speak with you about this incident?
3. What are the possible long-term consequences of this incident?
4. What strategies will you employ to deal with relations among members of the school community?

Suggested Activity

Review the policies and resources available for assisting faculty and staff in dealing with issues of diversity in your district and school. Read current professional literature dealing with such issues and outline a plan that you believe would reduce the chances of an incident like the one described occurring in your school community.

Problem 57: The Southern Belle—
An Ineffective Teacher with Strong Ties to the Community

Note: The following case study was submitted by graduate students Harriet Waller and Chris Cale and edited by Lynette Fields.

You are a principal who is new to the school. Ms. Belle has been the reading teacher at your school for twenty-five years. She knows most of the people in the community and has taught the parents of her current students. Most of the community has a begrudging respect for her and often visit her and send her homemade treats.

The previous administration found Ms. Belle to be set in her ways and difficult to change. She refused to teach from the new textbooks and continued using the same lessons from when she first started teaching.

When confronted, her rationale was "if it ain't broke, don't fix it." The previous administration gave up and left her to herself. Ms. Belle always received satisfactory evaluations.

The first problem that you notice as the new principal is that Ms. Belle is always late for team meetings. The first two times, you note her lateness, but on the third time, you remind her how important the meetings are.

The second problem that arises is the implementation of a new districtwide policy regarding the uniformity of the reading curriculum. Ms. Belle did not attend any of the training sessions and declares that she has produced successful students in the past so she is not going to implement the new program.

When you confront Ms. Belle with your concerns, she has "fainting spells." She claims that she is unable to finish the discussion because she is getting upset and feels faint. As she rushes out of the door, she says, "You should be ashamed of yourself, harassing me this way. You must know that I will call my friends and supporters in the community, who are willing to go to the media if necessary to expose your harassment of an elderly teacher." With that, she slams the door behind her.

Case Questions

1. How will you deal with the two specific problems thus far with Ms. Belle: her lateness and her refusal to implement the district curriculum?
2. What is your long-term plan for working with Ms. Belle?
3. How can you protect yourself from being accused of age discrimination?
4. How will you handle supporters of Ms. Belle in the community?
5. How will you deal with unfavorable media if Ms. Belle succeeds in getting them involved?

Suggested Activity

Create a list of strategies that you would use to be proactive and defensive in protecting your professional reputation for situations similar to this one.

Problem 58: Up in Smoke—Assistant Principals Deal with a Potential Bomb and a Teacher Who Lacks Common Sense

You are an assistant principal. Your principal is at a conference several hours away. As you arrive at school, one of the secretaries who opens the school each morning rushes to meet you at your car. She says that she has found something suspicious taped to the main doors and that she is scared to touch it. You hurry to take a look. The suspicious item looks like a bomb with a timer. There are other employees on campus: cafeteria workers and your head plant manager. It is 6:30 AM. Teachers typically begin arriving at 7:00 AM. Students who walk to campus or are dropped off by their parents begin arriving around 7:15 AM. Buses arrive around 7:30 AM. You have an open, unfenced campus, so anyone can walk up from any direction. There is another school six blocks from your school.

As your mind is racing, Ms. Petty, one of the teachers, approaches you. Ms. Petty is an effective second-year teacher. She is unaware of the problem. She is taking her class on a field trip today. She is concerned because one of her chaperones has backed out at the last minute. When you tell her that there is a potential bomb on the main doors that you need to deal with immediately, she begins to repeat her problem about the field trip.

Case Questions

1. At this moment, how do impress upon Ms. Petty the seriousness of the bomb situation?
2. What will you do about the field trip?
3. Within a few days, will you address this issue with Ms. Petty? If so, how?
4. In regard to dealing with the bomb, what do you do first?
5. How do you protect the employees who are already on campus?
6. How can you use these same employees to help you with this situation?
7. How do you protect employees and students who are arriving on campus?
8. How can you communicate with parents so that they do not drop their children off or come near the school?

9. How do you communicate with the buses to prevent them from dropping students off at your school?
10. How can you utilize the school close to your school?
11. When do you call the district office? Who do you call at the district office?

Suggested Activities

1. Create a crisis management plan to deal with situations that could affect the start-up or dismissal part of the school day. Include strategies for communicating and working with teachers.
2. Create a media plan for emergencies. Include strategies for using the media to communicate emergency information. Also describe the plan for dealing with unwanted media who swarm your campus in the event of a crisis.

Problem 59: Bad Moon Rising—Students' Public Misbehavior Creates the Wrong Perception of School Discipline

You are the new principal at a large middle school in a rural-to-suburban district. Within the community, the school has a long-standing reputation for disruptive student behavior and an uneven application of consequences for infractions of school rules, based on the "Who's your daddy?" principle. While discipline referrals and suspensions are down 30 percent since the implementation of a teacher-developed behavior management plan and rank among the best in the district, the perception among teachers and community members is still that the administration is doing little to manage discipline and that the students in the school are out of control. The issue of altering public perception is a frequent topic in administrative staff meetings, but efforts to highlight student accomplishments increase community involvement in school activities and the other long-range strategies have not appeared to have much of an impact on public opinion. That the local media, led by the editor of the local paper, see it as their duty to detail every event that reinforces the negative images of the school population that persist does not make the job easier.

One afternoon during the bus ride home, two students, rising to the challenge presented by their peers, moon passing motorists. The bus driver is unaware of the incident at the time but learns about it in the checkout line at the local supermarket that evening. One student has a history of questionable behavioral decisions and a dismal academic record, and his discipline record reflects several incidents of class tardiness and insubordination. The other student has a reputation for instigating fights and for malicious incidents directed toward teachers in the school, though he has never been caught. He has also had numerous run-ins with the local police but has never been prosecuted. His academic record is solid, and his father is the president of the Parent-Teacher Association and a close friend of the superintendent. The incident is reported to the local paper and is front-page news the following morning, along with an article that details incidents of other discipline issues at the school. Along with numerous phone messages from concerned parents and media requests for information, you receive a message from the superintendent that simply says, "Handle it!"

Case Questions

1. What immediate steps would you take to "handle" media relations in this situation?
2. What factors will need handling, and how will you prioritize them?
3. What avenues of communication are available to you? How would you use them?
4. How will you balance issues of student privacy rights and the school community's need to know that discipline policies are enforced fairly and consistently?
5. What long-term steps would you recommend to address the public perception problems?

Suggested Activity

Talk with the public information officer for your school district about how to plan for an interview with the local news media, and then create your own plan using the scenario given as the context. What types of questions should you anticipate? How will you frame your responses? What would you want the public to learn from your interview? What might the public want to know? What are the three most important talking points you would emphasize?

Problem 60: Excessive Edward—A Principal Who Is Overbearing

You are a new superintendent of a school district. The first week that you are in office, several upset parents call you and other district administrators. They are complaining about Mr. Marvin White, a high school principal. Mr. White has the philosophy that a principal's job is to run a tight ship in regard to student discipline. Mr. White believes that you "tell the children what you want and if they don't follow directions, you take swift action."

Many of the phone calls that you receive pertain to an incident that occurred this week in regard to student cars and parking on school grounds. According to the parents, Mr. White had made an announcement that students needed to buy their parking passes by the end of the week—at which time, Mr. White then walked through the school parking lot during school hours and removed the license plate on any student car that was without a pass. As a result, two students were pulled over by the local police department.

Other complaints revolved around Mr. White's interrogation of good students. When Mr. White perceived that drugs were on campus or that a fight was going to occur, he randomly called in good students and interviewed them for at least an hour in an attempt to get information. According to the parents, their children had no knowledge related to these situations and were pressured in an uncomfortable way by Mr. White. Parents also resented that their children were missing valuable class time.

Case Questions

1. What do you say to the parents in regard to their concerns?
2. How do you investigate these situations?
3. How do you research the possibility of past problems with Mr. White?

4. During your investigation, at what point do you talk with Mr. White? What do you say to him?
5. How can you effectively utilize electronic and printed news media to articulate the district's vision, mission, and priorities in regard to the concerns of the parents and students?
6. How can you respond effectively to electronic and printed news media if the concerned parents and students go to the local news organizations?

Suggested Activity

Imagine that you are the principal in the given situation and that your superintendent has given you this directive. Create a family-community involvement plan for your school so that appropriate policy development can occur. Write a summary of your family-community involvement plan.

REFLECTIVE QUESTIONS

1. What power structures exist in your district and community?
2. What are the vision, mission, and priorities of your school district?
3. What strategies will you use to effectively communicate to various groups in the community?
4. How will you build community support for your school or district?
5. What professional development do you need to better your skills in the area of news media?

CHAPTER 11

Ethical Law, Public Policy, and Political Systems

Educational Leadership Constituent Council Standard 11—Educational Law, Public Policy, and Political Systems specifies that the program prepares school leaders who demonstrate an understanding of and the capacity to apply knowledge of federal and state constitutional, statutory, and regulatory provisions, as well as judicial decisions governing education; apply knowledge of common law and contractual law requirements and procedures in an educational setting; define and relate the general characteristics of internal and external political systems as they apply to the school setting; describe the processes by which the federal, state, district, and school-site policies are formulated, enacted, implemented, and evaluated and develop strategies for influencing policy development; make decisions based on the moral and ethical implications of policy options and political strategies; analyze the major philosophical tenets of contemporary intellectual movements and analyze their effects on school contexts; and develop appropriate procedures and relationships for working with local governing boards.

As an administrator, you will find that much of what you do is highly prescribed and regulated but that there are complex decisions that fail to fall neatly into the situations imagined by policymakers. As a leader at the school or district level, you must understand not only the letter of the law but the nuances created by societal values, differing individual interpretations of policy, and the dilemmas created when following the letter of the law seems to violate its spirit. Most important, you will be called on to make decisions that affect the physical, emotional, and educational well-being of students for whom and to whom you are responsible.

What will you do when a teacher fails to provide a safe environment in which students can learn and grow? How will you deal with situations in which well-meaning faculty and staff unwittingly overstep their bounds or fail to safeguard student rights? Will you be prepared to address unethical behaviors on the parts of colleagues or superiors? Knowing the laws and policies that govern your actions is only part of the equation. The effective administrator must apply his or her knowledge consistently, impartially, and responsibly to safeguard the students, faculty, and staff that they serve. Honoring contractual obligations, mediating and rectifying errors and lapses in judgment, and formulating and implementing effective policies are among the skills that the administrator's job requires of its holder.

In this chapter you will be asked to consider situations in which these emerging knowledge, skills, and dispositions are put to the test. How will you develop as an effective leader? You will be called on to make reasoned judgments, negotiate positive outcomes in the midst of seemingly unsolvable conflict, and assume the role of advocate for students and teachers. To do so, you will learn to build relationships with governing boards, read and interpret policy in a fair and consistent manner, and gather relevant information to inform your actions. As you read and respond to these scenarios, think about how your legal responsibilities relate to your moral and ethical responsibilities as an educational leader. It is in distilling those understandings that you develop your personal code of professional standards that supplement and complement those prescribed by your district, your state, and your profession.

Problem 61: Welcome to Wild Kingdom—
A Teacher Who Does Not Teach or Supervise His Students

You are the principal of a high school. Three different teachers have complained to you about Mr. Hodges. They say that he has terrible classroom management and that the noise coming from his classroom makes it difficult to teach their own students. Mr. Hodges is a second-year English teacher and is one of the assistant football coaches. You begin to stop by his classroom at least once a day. Each time that you visit his classroom, you find him sitting at his desk. His students are loud and running around the classroom. When the students see you, they sit down and become quiet. After the third visit where students are visibly off task and not being managed, you conference with Mr. Hodges about his lack of supervision and classroom management. The next time that you visit Mr. Hodges, you find four of his students roaming the halls. When you return the students to Mr. Hodges, he has the class engaged in oral reading. After school, you conference with Mr. Hodges again and write a summary of the conference. You explain to him that having the students engaged in oral reading is a positive step, but you are concerned about the four students who were unsupervised in the hallway. You tell Mr. Hodges that you will cover his class tomorrow so that he can observe Mr. Proudfoot, another English teacher who has excellent classroom management. A week later during the school day, you receive an emergency call on your two-way radio. A student in Mr. Hodges's class is injured. When you arrive, you find a student with a broken arm. When you investigate the situation, you find that Mr. Hodges had three boys from his class go to the football field to move equipment so that it would be ready for practice. One of the boys climbed on top of the football goal, fell, and broke his arm.

Case Questions

1. What type of disciplinary consequence is appropriate for Mr. Hodges at this point?
2. Do the parents of the student with the broken arm have grounds for a lawsuit? If so, on what grounds?
3. How do you protect yourself and your school district?
4. What is your long-term plan for working with Mr. Hodges?
5. Do you plan to keep Mr. Hodges as a coach? Why or why not?

Suggested Activity

Write a two- to three-page paper in which you describe what negligence is, what prerequisites must exist for the courts to take action for negligence, and what the best defenses against negligence are.

Problem 62: Invasive Iven—A Teacher Who
Used Poor Judgment during Search and Seizure

You are the principal of a school. One of your teachers, Iven Pet-rosky, has been teaching at your school for five years. He is an average teacher who has not committed any type of disciplinary infraction nor received an unsatisfactory teaching evaluation during his career. In regard to student discipline, Mr. Petrosky has a pet peeve. He does not like for his students to chew gum in class. To his credit, Mr. Petrosky communicates this policy well to students and parents, and when students chew gum, Mr. Petrosky handles the infraction on his own, usually by calling the parents. Today Mr. Petrosky marches a student, Demetrious Boone, into your office. Mr. Petrosky and Demetrious are both visibly upset and angry with each other. Mr. Petrosky explains that he knows that Demetrious was chewing gum and that Demetrious is always playing games, wasting Mr. Petrosky's time. Demetrious says that he did not have gum and that he does not appreciate Mr. Petrosky putting his hands in his mouth. You ask Demetrious to elaborate, and he says that Mr. Petrosky physically pulled out Demetrious's tongue and moved it from side to side looking for the gum. Mr. Petrosky also touched the roof of the student's mouth.

Case Questions

1. What do you say to Demetrious Boone?
2. What do you say to the teacher?
3. Was this incident a legal search and seizure? Why or why not?
4. Was this incident battery? Why or why not?
5. Who will call Demetrious's parents? What should the parents be told?

Suggested Activities

1. Write a policy for appropriate search and seizure of students and their property that you could place in your school's teacher handbook. Describe how you would implement and evaluate this policy.

2. Write a letter of reprimand for Mr. Petrosky regarding this incident, following your district and state policies.

Problem 63: Should I Tell? Principles of Professional Conduct Where a Teacher Struggles with Confidentiality

Assume that you are a teacher and an athletic director at a large senior high school in Florida. You were instrumental in hiring one of your college classmates and friends from another district. She is an excellent teacher, and she coaches three sports for the high school athletic program. Your friend has been on the job for a few months, and she comes to you in a fit of rage. She makes you promise that you will not tell anyone what she is about to tell you. She makes you swear to silence. You listen and seek to understand what has her so upset.

The teacher-coach informs you that one of the male math teachers told one of the volleyball athletes that he will give her a passing grade if she has sexual relations with him. The volleyball player was an all-American last year and helped the volleyball team win the state championship title, the first in the school's history. As the story unfolds, you realize that there is a preponderance of evidence that this story is true. However, you have promised your longtime friend that you would not say a word about this to anyone.

Before answering the case questions and conducting the suggested activities, review the following principles of professional conduct for the education profession in your state. As an example, a few of the principles of professional conduct in the state of Florida have been provided for this case. Violation of any of these principles shall subject the individual to revocation or suspension of the individual educator's certificate or the other penalties as provided by law:

Obligation to the student requires that the individual: (a) Shall make reasonable effort to protect the student from conditions harmful to learning and/or to the student's mental and/or physical health and/or safety; (b) Shall not unreasonably restrain a student from independent action in pursuit of learning; (c) Shall not unreasonably deny a student access to diverse points of view; (d) Shall not intentionally suppress or distort subject matter relevant to a student's academic program; (e) Shall not intentionally expose a student to unnecessary embarrassment or disparagement; (f) Shall not intentionally violate or deny a student's legal rights; (g) Shall not harass or discriminate against any student on the basis of race, color, religion, sex, age, national or ethnic origin, political beliefs, marital status, handicapping condition, sexual orientation, or social and family background and shall make reasonable effort to assure that each student is protected from harassment or discrimination; (h) Shall not exploit a relationship with a student for personal gain or advantage; and (i) Shall keep in confidence personally identifiable information obtained in the course of professional service, unless disclosure serves professional purposes or is required by law.

Obligation to the public requires that the individual: (a) Shall take reasonable precautions to distinguish between personal views and those of any educational institution or organization with which the individual is affiliated; (b) Shall not intentionally distort or misrepresent facts concerning an educational matter in direct or indirect public expression; (c) Shall not use institutional privileges for personal gain or advantage; (d) Shall accept no gratuity, gift, or favor that might influence professional judgment; and (e) Shall offer no gratuity, gift, or favor to obtain special advantages.

Obligation to the profession of education requires that the individual: (a) Shall maintain honesty in all professional dealings; (b) Shall not interfere with a colleague's exercise of political or civil rights and responsibilities; (c) Shall not engage in harassment or discriminatory conduct which unreasonably interferes with an individual's performance of professional or work responsibilities or with the orderly processes of education or which creates a hostile, intimidating, abusive, offensive, or oppressive environment; and, further, shall make reasonable effort to assure that each individual is protected from such harassment or discrimination; (d) Shall not make malicious or intentionally false statements about a colleague; (e) Shall not use coercive means or promise special treatment to influence professional judgments of colleagues; (f) Shall report to appropriate authorities any known allegation of a violation of the Florida School Code or State Board of Education Rules; (g) Shall comply with the conditions of an order of the Education Practices Commission; (h) Shall, as the supervising administrator, cooperate with the Education Practices Commission in monitoring the probation of a subordinate. Specific Authority 229.053(1), 231.546(2)(b) FS. Law Implemented 231.546(2), 231.28 FS. History: New 7-6-82, Amended 12-20-83, Formerly 6B-1.06, Amended 8-10-92, 12-29-98.

Case Questions

1. As the teacher and athletic director, should you have promised the teacher-coach that you would not share the communication with anyone? Please explain.
2. What obligations do these educators have to the student?
3. What obligations do these educators have to the public?
4. What obligations do these educators have to the profession?
5. As the teacher and athletic director, what do you do now?
6. What will you say to the teacher-coach?

Suggested Activities

Using a systems perspective to the ethical, legal, policy, and political implications of this case, address the following activities and develop them fully, based on the case information provided:

1. What in-service training can be provided to employees that will give them the knowledge and skills necessary to act in accordance with legal and ethical policies that govern schools as political systems?
2. Discuss and explain the specific principles of professional conduct that have been provided and are applicable to this case.
3. Write a two- to three-page paper about sexual harassment of students. Answer the following questions:
   a. How do the courts define sexual harassment?
   b. What are the two basic categories of behavior that constitute sexual harassment under Title IX?
   c. What may happen to a school district as a system when there is a violation of Title IX?
   d. Describe three cases of the U.S. Supreme Court that deal with sexual harassment.

Problem 64: Manifestation Destiny—
Student Discipline and the Individualized Education Plan

You are a principal of an elementary school with a diverse population, including students for whom English is a second language, students with learning and behavioral disabilities, and students who have difficulty following school and classroom rules and procedures. Several weeks into the first semester, a third grader named Ryan transfers into your school. His academic records from his previous school, in a neighboring county, have been slow to arrive, but you have gotten to know Ryan well during his short time in the building.

Ryan has presented his teachers with behavioral challenges since the day his grandmother enrolled him. Your assistant principal has worked closely with the teachers to calm his frequent tantrums and address the aggressive and defiant behaviors, which range from displaying his genitalia to his female classmates to defacing the restrooms and stealing ice cream in the cafeteria at lunchtime. To modify his behaviors, his teachers have used traditional behavior management strategies, such as time-outs, phone conferences with his grandmother, and placing him in an alternative classroom for a day. After sessions with the guidance counselor and repeated requests for assistance from the teachers—and after his last violent outburst, in which he broke the nose of a teacher who was trying to restrain him during a fight that he had instigated—your assistant principal resorted to a three-day suspension and required a face-to-face conference with the grandmother before reinstating Ryan.

On the day of the conference, your secretary comes into your office and tells you that the assistant principal needs your immediate assistance in the conference room. Ryan's grandmother has arrived for the conference with an advocate from a local group who provides support to families of children with disabilities. Apparently, they have brought with them a copy of Ryan's individualized education plan (IEP) and copies of several other records that his previous school has not yet forwarded. Among the documents is his discipline record, which indicates that he had been suspended from school for a cumulative total of ten days in his previous school. According to your secretary, she heard the words "least restrictive environment," "manifestation hearing," and "due process" being discussed as she was sent to find you.

Case Questions

1. What are the immediate legal issues that you must address related to Ryan's diagnosed disabilities?

2. What are your school's liabilities and responsibilities at this point?
3. What information do you need to plan your course of action?
4. What resources can you call on to assist you in addressing the needs of the student and any potential legal difficulties related to this situation?
5. What might your staff have done to head off this situation before it became a matter of noncompliance with a child's IEP?

Suggested Activities

1. Review your school district's policies and procedures for implementing IEPs and consider whether or not they are reasonably calculated to prevent a situation like the one detailed here. If so, write a policy brief indicating how and why they are adequate. If not, make a series of recommendations for changes in the policy that might prevent such an occurrence.
2. Prepare a brief presentation with handouts that would assist the staff and faculty in your school in identifying potential problems such as the one described and making them aware of your school district's relevant policies and procedures.

Problem 65: The Good Ol' Boy's Use of Petty Cash—
A Principal Who Oversteps His Bounds

You are the assistant principal in an upper-class school district that is one of the top-paying districts in the state. Landing a job in this district was a blessing for you and your family. However, you came from outside the area and have never truly been accepted by the "good ol' boy network" within the organizational structure of the district.

You have a strong background in school finance and school law, which are two areas where your principal is weak. Your principal is close friends with the administrators in the central office, including the superintendent and several powerful school board members. This group is often found socializing and playing golf together several times a week.

Your principal instructs you to purchase from a local company a midsized trailer that is large enough to carry four of the school's golf carts. He instructs you to use petty cash to make the purchase. As part of your due diligence, you inquire about the need for such a trailer, when the school has gone years without one. Your principal tells you that this local company will sell this trailer to the school for a good price (less than $1,500). He goes on to say that the trailer will be used to carry the golf carts to and from the service center for annual maintenance service. He also states that the groundskeepers could use it during the year to help them with their work.

The principal's request and explanation do not sit well with you, and you want to be sure that you are defensible in carrying out this directive. You look up the policy that governs the use of petty cash. In Florida, it is as follows:

Petty cash funds may be authorized by the school board pursuant to adopted policy for the purpose of making small expenditures for operation of schools. Each fund must be authorized by the school board as to the amount and the specific person responsible for the fund. The amount of a petty cash fund shall be commensurate with the volume and the purpose of transactions, but in no case shall exceed one thousand (1,000) dollars. (2) Petty cash funds shall be accounted for separately from all other funds maintained at the individual school center or other locations authorized by the school board. (3) The school board may reimburse each authorized petty cash fund as often as necessary upon the presentation of receipts equal to the amount of the requested reimbursement. At no time shall these funds be used as a loan or advancement to any organization or person, including cashing of personal checks. (4) Each petty cash fund must be replenished prior to the closing of records for the fiscal year in order that all expenditures shall be recorded for that year; provided, however, that where school centers are completely closed for the eleventh or twelfth month, each petty cash fund may be deposited into the school's internal funds bank account if authorized by the district school board in a rule or returned to the school board on or before the close of the school year and may be reestablished at the beginning of the subsequent school year upon authorization of the school board. Specific Authority 229.053(1), 237.02(1)(c) FS. Law Implemented 237.02 FS. History: New 4-11-70, Amended 9-17-72, 12-18-72, Repromulgated 12-5-74, Formerly 6A-1.57, Amended 4-18-89, 8-15-94.

You confront the principal about his request to purchase the trailer because it violates several aspects of the legal statute. He tells you not to worry, that he is connected to the internal and external politically powerful people, and that this will be okay. Fearing that you might lose your job, you comply with this request. A week after the trailer was purchased, you see your principal and his pals riding out of town with two of their personal golf carts and two school golf carts loaded onto the trailer, with golf clubs strapped to the back of each cart.

Case Questions

1. Will you say anything to your principal? Please explain.
2. Will the political connections of your principal to the internal and external systems protect you and your actions?
3. Do you believe that the principal knowingly asked you to violate the statute?
4. How might you use the policy and statutes to protect your actions?
5. Do you believe that the principal knew or cared about how the citizens and business agencies might perceive this, if they found out?
6. How might this affect your future?
7. List some of the ethical problems that this case presents.

Suggested Activity

Write a three-page paper where you explain how a new administrator coming into an existing organizational culture can best understand internal and external political systems and how he or she can deal with possible illegal or unethical pressures from members of such systems.

Problem 66: Evolving Controversy—Secular Humanism Meets Religious Conservatism in the Science Lab

You are the principal of a secondary school (grades 7–12) in a conservative rural Southern farming community. You emerge from your office one morning to investigate an apparent commotion in the front office. You witness a group of parents and students squaring off in a shouting match in the middle of the lobby. After a few moments, it is clear that the heated debate centers on the science curriculum taught in the seventh and ninth grades. Your seventh-grade life science classes are taught by Fred, a veteran teacher with deep roots in the community. He is a deacon in his local church, and you have overheard him discussing his fundamental religious beliefs in the faculty lounge room on more than one occasion. The ninth-grade biology classes are taught by Summer, a young Ivy League graduate who came to your school as part of a special federal program designed to help economically challenged communities such as yours attract qualified teachers in high-need content areas.

You are aware of a continuing controversy in the county related to the introduction of irradiated seeds and genetically altered crop samples planted by local farmers struggling to stay economically solvent. You know that the conservative spiritual leaders in the community have objected to these experimental crops on religious grounds and publicly condemn these farmers from their pulpits. As of today, the community controversy and animosity has spilled over into your school setting, with parents and students drawing the line between what they see as secular humanism and religious conservatism. Half of the parents are angry that Fred presents creationism as an equivalent theory to evolution; the other half are angered that Summer merely mentions it as an alternative theory, concentrating instead on evolution as outlined in the state curriculum standards and county curriculum guide.

Case Questions

1. How do you diffuse the immediate conflict? What do you say to the assembled parents?
2. What will inform the position you take on this issue?
3. What issues must be resolved within the science department and within the school?
4. To what extent should local interests and values influence the curriculum taught in a public school?
5. Which teacher is doing the right thing? How do you know?

Suggested Activity

Investigate the federal, state, and local statutes as well as any relevant case law and board policy in your district that address curricular issues such as the teaching of evolution. Who has the right to define curriculum? To what extent do individual teachers have a right to alter the prescribed curriculum to address community values and concerns? What are your responsibilities as an administrator with regard to teacher-implemented mandated curriculum? Write a policy brief that would inform a new administrator in your district and assist him or her in addressing similar situations.

Problem 67: Categorical Program Funds and a Superintendent Who Is Dishonest

You are a new assistant principal in a school district that has an elected superintendent. Your principal worked hard to get the current superintendent elected to her four-year term. It is time for the superintendent to run for reelection. The superintendent schedules a visit to see you and your principal.

The superintendent engages in small talk for several minutes and then gets to the point of her visit. She and the financial officer for the district recently checked the categorical budgets of all schools and discovered that your school has a surplus in the civic/public relations fund. She reminds your principal that categorical program funds that are not expended by a school at the close of a fiscal year cannot be carried forward to the next fiscal year. She encourages your principal to spend this money with the county commissioners' initiative to annex the city (a project that she has supported from the beginning) within the next few weeks. Being a loyal supporter and close friend of the superintendent, your principal assures her that this will be taken care of right away. She thanks both of you for your support and leaves the office.

You recall from your law course in your administrative preparation program that the superintendent may have misrepresented the truth about the use of categorical program funds. You go back to your

Florida law book and ascertain that your intuition was correct—the superintendent did misrepresent the truth. In fact, the law states:

> Categorical program funds, identified in Section 236.081, Florida Statutes, or any other earmarked funds allocated to a school district shall be expended only in the program for which funds are provided. Any such funds, except those categorical program funds provided through contract or grant for a specific period of time, not expended by a school district as of the close of a fiscal year shall be carried forward into the following fiscal year for the same categorical purpose. Specific Authority 229.053 FS. Law Implemented 236.081, 237.01 FS. History: New 10-31-74, Repromulgated 12-5-74, Amended 4-8-75, Formerly 6A-1.141.

Case Questions

1. How will you deal with the discrepancy of information?
2. Do you believe that the superintendent knew that she misrepresented the truth?
3. Do you believe that the principal knew that the superintendent was wrong?
4. Why would the superintendent ask the principal to spend the money with a local governing board in which she was closely aligned?
5. How might this affect your principal's future?
6. Predict how the school board members might view this incident.
7. List some of the ethical problems this case presents.

Suggested Activity

Write a two- to three-page paper explaining how school leaders such as superintendents and principals should develop appropriate procedures and relationships for working with local governing boards.

Problem 68: No Win on Zero Tolerance— A Principal Caught in the Middle

You are a principal of a high school in a suburban community. Recent growth in your area has created the impression among many community members that student discipline and school safety needs are different, now that a more racially, ethnically, and economically diverse group of students are attending local schools. Your school district has implemented a zero-tolerance policy for drugs, alcohol, and weapons, consistent with federal and state legislative mandates. This policy allows for the superintendent and the school board to exercise discretion in enforcement to avoid incidents like the highly publicized case in a nearby district where a student was expelled for bringing an aspirin to school following root canal surgery.

Recently, in response to community pressures, the school board members have taken an increasingly hard line on cases involving violations of these policies. The school board chair, Ms. Smith, has been quoted in the local media saying, "Zero means zero, and we need to send a message that those people won't change who we are in this community." The superintendent, Mr. Jones, has continued to advocate for consideration of cases on an individual basis, citing issues of age, intent, severity of offense, and mitigating circumstances as considerations in making decisions about suspensions and expulsions. The debate has recently hit close to home.

Tad Martin, an honors student in his senior year with a scholarship offer from a major university, borrowed his father's car on Monday. As Tad and his friends were stowing their books in the car before after-school practice, one of young men noticed a hunting rifle in the trunk. Tad took the weapon away from his friend, explaining that his father had been hunting over the weekend and had obviously forgotten to take his gun into the house on his return. In response to questions from his friends, Tad picks up the rifle and demonstrates how to site and aim the rifle. Another student several cars away and a teacher on bus duty see Tad with the rifle, apparently aiming it in the direction of other students. The school resource officer is summoned, and Tad is immediately arrested.

Word travels through the community, and shortly after you arrive at school on Tuesday, you receive a call from Ms. Smith of the school board. She demands that you publicly support her position in this matter and press for the maximum penalty for this recent transfer from the neighboring metropolitan area. "They have to know we won't put up with them coming here and making our schools as unsafe as theirs," she says. "We'll be watching you." As you hang up, your phone rings again. This time it is Superintendent Jones, who asks that you do what you can with the witnesses to help present the case in a light that is favorable to the student and would justify leniency in the disposition of the case. After all, he says, "This is a kid with a bright future and a state championship game next week. There could be real fallout in the community if we take away his chance for a shot at college and an athletic career." You hang up the phone and sit quietly for a moment, caught between the proverbial rock and hard place. What will you do?

Case Questions

1. What are your legal and ethical responsibilities in this case?
2. How will you respond to the conflicting expectations of the superintendent and school board chair?
3. What policies and other considerations will inform your response to the incident and your conversations with your superiors?
4. How will you handle this incident with your faculty, students, and community?
5. What are the possible intended and unintended consequences of following the advice of Ms. Smith or Mr. Jones?
6. What other options do you have available to you?

Suggested Activity

Investigate the discipline policies in your district as they apply to decisions involving cases covered by the Safe and Drug-Free Schools Act, and revisit your personal educational philosophy. Assuming the facts presented in this case, prepare for and role-play a conference with the school board chair and with the superintendent. In your simulated meetings, outline what you believe to be an equitable solution to the situation and one that will allow you to maintain a positive working relationship with each for the remainder of your tenure as an administrator in the district. Then debrief with a colleague about your stance and your role-playing scenario.

REFLECTIVE QUESTIONS

1. What do you believe to be the areas of school law that are most commonly litigated today?

2. Of the areas listed in answer to question 1, to what extent are they related to provisions of the U.S. Constitution?

3. Of the areas listed in answer to question 1, how does your state's statutes compare and contrast to U.S. Supreme Court findings?

4. What is your awareness level of internal and external political systems that affect school leaders in your school district? How can you gain knowledge of these systems?

5. How are policies developed in your school district?

6. Describe the local governing boards that principals in your area routinely work with. How are processes and relationships established?

General Index

Topic Index

Note: Numbers refer to chapter problems (case studies), not page numbers.

About the Authors

Lynette Fields, PhD, an instructor in educational leadership, joined the faculty at the University of South Florida, St. Petersburg, in 1999. She has authored numerous articles on classroom management issues in teacher education and topics related to administrator preparation. Her major research interest is studying the role of the assistant principal.

Brianne Reck, PhD, an assistant professor of educational leadership and curriculum studies, joined the faculty at the University of South Florida in 2002. One of her primary interests is developing innovative administrator preparation programs that address the changing nature of educational leadership in the context of high-stakes accountability for student achievement.

Robert Egley, PhD, is currently the principal of Clewiston High School in Hendry County, Florida. He has seventeen years as an administrator at the elementary, middle, and high school levels. Dr. Egley has written numerous articles on high-stakes testing, invitational education, and instructional leadership.